W9-BVA-008

DISCARDED

# Fabric of Faith

MT. PLEASANT PUBLIC LIBRARY
DISCARDED
IOWA

# Fabric of Faith

## A Guide to the Prayer Quilt Ministry

### KIMBERLY WINSTON

MOREHOUSE PUBLISHING

HARRISBURG / PENNSYLVANIA

Copyright © 2006 by Kimberly Winston

All rights reserved. No part of this book may be reproduced, stored in a retrieval system, or transmitted in any form or by any means, electronic, mechanical, including photocopying, recording, or otherwise, without the written permission of the publisher.

Unless otherwise noted, the Scripture quotations contained herein are from the New Revised Standard Version Bible, copyright © 1989 by the Division of Christian Education of the National Council of Churches of Christ in the U.S.A. Used by permission. All rights reserved.

Morehouse Publishing, P.O. Box 1321, Harrisburg, PA 17105
Morehouse Publishing, 445 Fifth Avenue, New York, NY 10016
Morehouse Publishing is an imprint of Church Publishing Incorporated.

Cover design: Brenda Klinger
Interior design: Beth Oberholtzer

**Library of Congress Cataloging-in-Publication Data**

Winston, Kimberly, 1964–
    Fabric of faith : a guide to the prayer quilt ministry / Kimberly Winston.
        p.    cm.
    Includes bibliographical references.
    ISBN-13: 978-0-8192-2193-3 (casebound)  1. Prayer—Christianity.  2. Quilting.
3. Quilts.  4. Church work.  I. Title.
BV210.3.W56    2006
248.4'6—dc22
                                                                                    2006005480

*Printed in the United States of America*

06 07 08 09    10 9 8 7 6 5 4 3 2

DISCARDED

For Wendy Mathson and Kathy Cueva,
whose vision began and continues to drive this ministry

For Kody,
without whom there would be no Prayer Quilt Ministry

For all the quilters and people who pray
whom I met during the reporting of this book.
May God continue to lead them to share
their talents and their compassion with others.

For my husband, Terry
who never doubts

# CONTENTS

# INTRODUCTION

*W*hen I was a small girl, I had a yellow quilt. Two pieces of yellow nylon polyester with some thin batting, framed by a narrow border of yellow satin. It was nothing special.

Except to me. To me, it was everything, and throughout the tiny tragedies and small miseries that occasionally disrupted my childhood, I kept that quilt by me. It had been given to me when I was a baby living in my grandmother's house in Ohio, a place where I always felt part of a family. When my mother and I moved hundreds of miles away, that quilt went with me. When I held it next to me, I always felt safe and loved. Every night, I spread its yellow thinness out on my bottom sheet and lay down on top of it. It was my good luck charm, my anchor, my home.

Why should a quilt have such talismanic power? Why should a quilt come to mean more than physical warmth and softness, and stand instead as a sanctuary and shield? Why should a quilt—a mere sandwich of fabric and stuffing—be more than, well, a quilt?

The truth is, it isn't. Not by itself. But when a quilt is imbued with meaning, reinforced with love, and given away with compassion, it can become a shelter in times of sickness, heartache, and uncertainty. Made with love, purpose, and hope, such a quilt can become an unbreakable link to the community that nurtures us and a tangible reminder that we are all bound up together in God's world.

That is the idea behind the Prayer Quilt Ministry, or, as it is often called, the Prayers & Squares Ministry. Under either banner, it is a non-denominational, interfaith ministry in which entire congregations—men, women, and children alike—contribute to the making of quilts that will be given away to people in crisis. These quilts are not quilted in the usual sense—three layers of fabric and batting held together by intricate and decorative stitches. Rather, they are "tied quilts," bound through by strands of cotton thread that are tied into square knots on the quilt's top. They are smaller than bed quilts—usually just big enough to wrap about someone shoulders or spread across their lap. They are made in colors and patterns as unique and individual as the people who make them and the people who receive them.

But the Prayer Quilt Ministry is not an excuse for quilting enthusiasts to get together and gossip over the quilting frame. What makes a quilt a prayer quilt is that it is made not just with artistry, but with purpose; not just with fabric, but with prayers. From the time the fabric is purchased to the time it is given away, a prayer quilt is prayed over by scores of people. The person who cuts the fabric prays. The person who sews the quilt top prays. The person who inserts the ties prays. And, most importantly, when the quilt is completed, it is placed before a congregation, and every member is invited to bind a tie and say a prayer for the person it will ultimately comfort. A quilt is a prayer quilt because prayers are, quite literally, part of its fabric.

Usually, the recipient of a prayer quilt is someone most of the people who have had a hand in its making do not know and will never meet. It is a quilt, then, made not just with cotton, but with compassion; not just with fabric, but

*Oh, God, make small*

*The old star-eaten blanket of the sky,*

*That I may fold it round me and in comfort lie.*

THOMAS ERNEST HULME*

with faith. A prayer quilt is the physical representation of the biblical principle "love thy neighbor."

And just as a prayer quilt holds prayers, it also holds stories—of the hopes and dreams of the people it comforts, of the lives that go on after a prayer quilt's work is done. There are as many of these stories as there are prayer quilts—thousands and thousands. In these pages, I tell the ones that most touched me when I heard them.

But this book is not for people who want to learn how to quilt or who want to add to their quilting skills. Rather, it is for those who want to become involved in the Prayer Quilt Ministry, either by starting a chapter in their own congregation, by joining an established chapter, or by bringing the practice of prayer to their quilting skills. It is also for people who would like to add some spiritual depth to their quilting by learning about the incredible power prayer can endow in a couple of pieces of cloth. This book is not about how to quilt; it is about how to pray. The Prayer Quilt Ministry is, in essence, a ministry of intercessory prayer—the act of praying not for one's self, but for others. You do not have to be a *quilter* to be involved in the Prayer Quilt Ministry. But you do have to be a *pray-er*. As one California prayer quilter once put it to me, "You don't have to be a quilter to be in this ministry. You just have to have a heart to serve."

And that is why my own yellow quilt was so special to me. It was a sign to me that I was loved, that I was cherished. It was a link to a community of people who believed in me and wanted the best for me. My yellow quilt was invested with the love of those who raised me, just as a prayer quilt is filled with the love and prayers of those who give it. My yellow quilt was a sign that I belonged. A prayer quilt is a sign that we all belong to each other. A prayer quilt says we are all part of God's family.

*Prayer is the fair and radiant daughter of all the human virtues, the arch connecting heaven and earth, the sweet companion that is alike the lion and the dove; and prayer will give you the key of heaven.*

HONORÉ DE BALZAC*

*It is comforting when one has a sorrow to lie in the warmth of one's bed and there, abandoning all effort and all resistance, to bury even one's head under the cover, giving one's self up to it completely, moaning like branches in the autumn wind. But there is still a better bed, full of divine odors. It is our sweet, our profound, our impenetrable friendship.*

<small>Marcel Proust*</small>

I have never needed a prayer quilt, thank goodness. Nor have I ever known anyone who received one. Again, thank goodness. So it is hard to accurately nail down the special nature of this thing that is so much more than just a blanket. How to really know what prayer quilts mean to the people who receive them? How to exactly describe the way a prayer quilt "works?" The best way is through the stories and words of those whose lives they have entered and changed.

STORY OF A QUILT
# *Mariah's Quilt*

Mariah battled a disease most children her age cannot pronounce, let alone comprehend. In 2001, when she was four years old, she was diagnosed with neuroblastoma, a serious form of childhood cancer.

It wasn't the first tragedy to come into the small girl's life. Her father was killed while working on a road construction project in Albuquerque, where Mariah still lives with her mother, Joy, and brother, Kevin.

At about the same time Mariah received her diagnosis, the women's group at Valley View United Methodist Church in Española, New Mexico, decided to start a chapter of Prayers & Squares. "We wanted to make quilts for people who were ill," said Elizabeth Martin, a church member whose granddaughter told her about Mariah. The little girl, they decided, would be the perfect candidate to receive their first quilt. "We were told her favorite color was purple, and we knew that butterflies were for hope," Elizabeth said. "So that was the material we chose—purple with butterflies."

The quilt was finished and blessed on the church altar during two services. After each service, church members tied knots, saying prayers for Mariah, her mother, and her brother.

Mariah was given a round of chemotherapy and radiation in Albuquerque, and sent to the University of California Los Angeles for another round of chemo and radiation and, ultimately, a bone marrow transplant that would include stem cell treatment. Across the miles, through all the pinpricks, tubes, and testing, her quilt stayed at her side.

Mariah is now eight years old, and her cancer is in remission. She has to wear thick glasses and hearing aids, but that hasn't kept her from being a cheerleader at her grade school. "I think that spunk saw her through along with many, many prayers," Elizabeth says.

"That is the story of our first quilt," Elizabeth says. "No wonder we have made and presented dozens more."

*One of the signs of passing youth is the birth of a sense of fellowship with other human beings as we take our place among them.*

VIRGINIA WOOLF*

# CHAPTER ONE
# WHY MAKE PRAYER QUILTS?

## Finding the Spirit in the Prayer Quilt Ministry

"There will never cease to be some in need on the earth."

—DEUTERONOMY 15:11

There are so many opportunities to give. We can write a check. We can share our time. We can just hold a hand and tell someone we're there when the darkest of nights descends.

So why make prayer quilts? Why take the time to buy some fabric, cut it into intricate little pieces, sew them together, and sandwich it with batting? Why spend all that energy to send something out into the world that won't feed anyone, clothe anyone, or change anyone's material circumstances?

Because prayer quilts are more than blankets. They are the visible, tangible physical evidence of faith—faith in God, faith in love, and faith in prayer. But perhaps most importantly, they're also a symbol of our faith in one another.

When we make a prayer quilt, we're declaring our belief that love for one another as children of God is so strong it can be a force for change. We're saying that God's love and our love are one and the same, and that together they can bring comfort, strength, joy, and healing.

We also make prayer quilts because they can serve as a powerful vehicle for spiritual growth and renewal—not just for the recipient in crisis, but also for the quilters themselves. Prayer quilts are vessels that hold all the good wishes, thoughts, and hopes—the prayers—of the people who make them. They carry those prayers to people who need them and literally wrap them up in those prayers. Think of that for a minute: What would it feel like to be enveloped in a warmth that's generated not only by layers of fabric and batting, but also by the hundreds of individual prayers that people, usually nameless strangers, made just for you in your specific situation? In times of need, a prayer quilt provides something doctors, nurses, and other caregivers may not be trained or prepared to give. A prayer quilt lets the recipient know that he or she is a part of God's glorious creation and, for that simple reason alone, has worth and merit and is deserving of love.

The prayer quilt is so much more than a pretty blanket. You can buy one of those anywhere. The prayer quilt is a touchable emblem of human kindness and a link to the source of that kindness—God.

Because a prayer quilt is a vessel of love and caring, it can be said to embody the universal philosophy that underpins all the world's great religious traditions: that God, called by many names, is about love. When we care for others, especially those we do not know, we are giving life to this immeasurable aspect of the divine. And when we make and give away a prayer quilt, we affirm that all human beings, no matter what name they call God, are united in their love for him and for each other.

*Now faith is the assurance of things hoped for, the conviction of things not seen.*

HEBREWS 11:1

True, the Prayer Quilt Ministry was started by Christians, members of a United Methodist church. But the ministry has never restricted those who can receive the quilts or those who can make the quilts to a single faith. Because of this—and because the Prayer Quilt Ministry is founded on the universal religious truth that God is love—it can bring holiness, hope, and understanding to believers of many different faiths.

## Christianity

A prayer quilt is an example of so many of the teachings of Jesus. On the simplest level, it fulfills his charge that we love our neighbors. When we give away prayer quilts, we're following in the steps of the Good Samaritan, whose parable illustrates Jesus' command:

> A man was going down from Jerusalem to Jericho, and fell into the hands of robbers, who stripped him, beat him, and went away, leaving him half dead. Now by chance a priest was going down that road; and when he saw him, he passed by on the other side. So likewise a Levite, when he came to the place and saw him, passed by on the other side. But a Samaritan while traveling came near him; and when he saw him, he was moved with pity. He went to him and bandaged his wounds, having poured oil and wine on them. Then he put him on his own animal, brought him to an inn, and took care of him. The next day he took out two denarii, gave them to the innkeeper, and said, "Take care of him; and when I come back, I will repay you whatever more you spend." (Luke 10:30–35)

Then Jesus asks, "Which of these three do you think proved a neighbor to the man who fell among the robbers?" A man replies, "The man who showed mercy on him," and Jesus responds, "Go and do likewise."

*When we feel love and kindness toward others, it not only makes others feel loved and cared for, but it helps us also to develop inner happiness and peace.*

The Dalai Lama

Those who need prayer quilts, robbed of health or solace or good fortune, are like the man who fell among the thieves. Jesus commends not the well-connected men who pass him by, but the Samaritan, a total stranger, who *took care of him*. When we make prayer quilts, we are exemplifying the Samaritan's compassion. He didn't need to know who the victim was. He only needed to know that he could help. When we make prayer quilts, we're responding to the needs of strangers, too, offering them the abilities and skills we possess—the skill to sew and the ability to pray. When we make and give away a prayer quilt, we're obeying Jesus' admonition to follow the Samaritan's example, and Jesus' wish that we "go and do likewise."

## Judaism

We can think of a prayer quilt as a piece of the mosaic in the Jewish idea of *tikkun olam*, translated from the Hebrew as "to perfect, or to fix, the world." Jews often interpret this idea as a call to action and social justice, a declaration that human beings have a responsibility to right the world's wrongs through moral actions and charitable deeds. Seen through this lens, the gift of a prayer quilt is not only a charitable deed, but also a community's attempt to repair whatever is broken in the recipient's world.

Prayer quilts also fit the Jewish concept of *tzedakah*—giving to the less fortunate, not just because we can, but because it is just and righteous to do so. The great twelfth-century Jewish rabbi and philosopher Maimonides said that *tzedakah* requires that the giver bestow not only with his hand, but also with his heart; not only of his wealth, but also of his compassion and empathy. Given in this spirit, a prayer quilt has the very essence of *tzedakah* woven into its fabric.

The Jewish sages taught that the world rests on three pillars: the Temple, the Torah (Jewish scriptures), and *gemilut hasadim*, or acts of lovingkindness.

*If there is among you anyone in need, a member of your community in any of your towns within the land that the Lord your God is giving you, do not be hard-hearted or tight-fisted toward your needy neighbor. You should rather open your hand, willingly lending enough to meet the need, whatever it may be.*

DEUTERONOMY 15:7–8

Among these is *bikkur holim*, the visiting and comforting of the sick. Judaism teaches that tending to the spiritual and physical needs of the ill is a *mitzvah*, a good deed. So when we make and give a prayer quilt, we're not only helping to relieve the pain and suffering of those who are ill, but we are doing something to make the world a better and more holy place.

## Islam

In Islam, Muslims are commanded to do acts of charity in order to be considered true Muslims. Called *zakat*, it is one of the Five Pillars of Islam and a law a good Muslim must abide by. There are many forms of *zakat*, and a prayer quilt is probably most like *sadaqah*, a freewill, charitable offering. In the Qu'ran, the Islamic holy book, Allah, or God, says that an act of *sadaqah* will be returned to the giver many times over:

> Let those who give alms, both men and women, and lend unto Allah a goodly loan, it will be doubled for them, and theirs will be a rich reward.
>
> —Qur'an 57:18

Good deeds, like the making and giving of a prayer quilt, are *sadaqah*.

> God is never unjust
> In the least degree
> If there is any good done,
> He doubleth it,
> And giveth from his own
> Presence a great reward.
> —Qur'an 4:40

*You cannot believe in GOD until you believe in yourself.*

Sri Swami
Vivekananda,
Hindu mystic

The Qur'an also teaches that *sadaqah* "purifies" the giver in that it frees him or her from attachment to material goods. "When we give, we are showing trust in God that God will provide for us," says Ingrid Mattson, a professor of Islamic studies at Hartford Seminary in Connecticut. The same can be said of giving a prayer quilt—when we give it to someone we are showing our trust that God will care and provide for them in their time of need.

## Buddhism

One of the tenets of the Buddhist tradition, of which there are many branches, is that human beings should strive to exemplify "The Four Noble Virtues": lovingkindness, compassion, equanimity, and joy in the happiness and well-being of others. What is a prayer quilt if not the perfect manifestation of these virtues? It is crafted out of compassion for another and is given with lovingkindness. We rejoice when recipients report that their circumstances have improved; we grieve with them and their loved ones when they do not. A prayer quilt also exemplifies the Buddha's teaching about the Eightfold Path, the route to Enlightenment. It upholds the concept of "right action," the demand that we behave selflessly, constructively, and harmlessly to all living things. The prayer quilt also illustrates the Buddhist concept of "right understanding," the belief that the world is a conditional and impermanent place. In the Buddhist idea of the world, the quilt cannot "cure" or "fix" recipients, but offers comfort and accompanies them to the next stage of their lives. It is a sign of the Buddhist belief that all life is impermanent.

*Teach this triple truth to all: A generous heart, kind speech, and a life of service and compassion are the things which renew humanity.*

THE BUDDHA

## Native American

When the first European colonists to the New World were stricken with hunger and disease, it was the Native Americans who gave what they had to keep the white men and women alive during those hard winters. This was because most Native American cultures consider it an honor to be able to give, as well as to receive. Native Americans also consider it vital that there be a "circle of giving"—that the recipient of a gift give something also, not necessarily back to the giver, but to someone else in need. This is a beautiful expression of the philosophy of the Prayer Quilt Ministry. Some of the most active Prayers & Squares chapters were started by those whose own lives were touched by the gift of a prayer quilt, who then made prayer quilts for others.

❧

So when we make a prayer quilt, we're not only living out the tenets of our own religion, whatever it may be. We're also in tune with the beliefs of others. There is no reason a prayer quilt cannot be made by people of one faith and given to someone of another, very different one. That's because the mechanism of the prayer quilt is *prayer,* the shared language we have with people of faiths not our own. It is through prayer, and prayer quilts, that we communicate and demonstrate our caring, love, and shared responsibility for one another. Whether we are Buddhist or Baha'i, Christian or Jewish, Zuni or Zoroastrian, we can all meet in the spirit and the power of prayer.

*The most eloquent prayer is the prayer through hands that heal and bless.*

BILLY GRAHAM**

# CHAPTER TWO

# A HISTORY OF THE PRAYER QUILT MINISTRY

## Kody's Quilt

"Certain thoughts are prayers. There are moments when, whatever be the attitude of the body, the soul is on its knees."

—VICTOR HUGO, *LES MISERABLES*

The Prayer Quilt Ministry began with a small boy whose name was Kody.

Kody was born in 1989 with a congenital heart defect, and lived with his granny, Carolyn Wright, in Poway, north of San Diego. In 1992, just a few days before his third birthday, Kody became very ill. His heart was failing, and he required immediate surgery. It did not go well. The blonde-haired boy slipped into a coma, and doctors gave his family little hope that he would survive.

Carolyn couldn't bear to see the little boy suffer. But there was nothing she could do for him at the hospital. So she called her friends in an informal quilting circle at her church, Hope United Methodist. She asked them to pray for the child and his family.

The quilters were moved by the boy's situation. Most had known him since he was born. They prayed. They talked. They wondered what they could do. Finally, someone in the group asked Wendy Mathson, a skilled quilter and fellow parishioner, how fast she could make a quilt. The thought was that a quilt made by people who loved Kody would comfort him. At the very least, it would bring a personal touch to his hospital room.

Wendy made the quilt top overnight, using some of the first blocks the group had made a few weeks before. It was patched in squares of school bus yellow, apple red, bright orange, and sky blue. But there was no time for the painstaking hand stitching that usually binds the top layer of a quilt to the bottom layer. Even machine stitching seemed like it would take too much time. So the Hope United Methodist quilters met in a church conference room to tie the layers together, piercing the quilt at regular intervals with strands of cotton thread and binding the layers with square knots.

As the women worked, bending their heads together over the small squares of patchwork, they were very quiet. The only sounds were the snip of the scissors on the ties. In the midst of the silence, one of the women spoke up. "Is everybody else praying?" she asked. Someone replied, "Yes," and another added, "There's got to be a prayer in every knot."

The prayer quilt was born.

The idea that a quilt could harbor prayers wasn't entirely foreign to Wendy. About a year before Kody became ill, she found herself in a deep state of prayer while making a quilt for a friend, a young girl in a body cast. As she quilted, she prayed for the girl's health. "The whole thing became very spiritual for me," Wendy says. "That was the seed being planted."

When Kody's prayer quilt was done, it was taken straight from the church to the hospital. "We felt it was so important that he be covered in prayers that

*We do pray for mercy,*
*And that same prayer*
*doth teach us all*
*to render*
*The deeds of mercy.*

WILLIAM SHAKESPEARE*

we wanted to get it to him right away," Wendy recalls. And Kody's response was immediate. "Even before he came to full consciousness, his hands were on the knots," Wendy remembers. "He was touching and pulling on the knots. We felt like this was him feeling our prayers." Soon, Kody began to improve, and eventually he emerged from his coma. His doctors and nurses saw how the prayer quilt affected Kody, and it touched them, too. As if he were writing a prescription, a doctor wrote in Kody's chart that his prayer quilt was to remain at his side throughout his hospital stay. "A needle stick, an X-ray, he always had his quilt," Wendy says.

Parents of other children in the same intensive care unit saw Kody's prayer quilt and asked if they, too, could have prayer quilts for their children. The quilters of Hope United Methodist said yes. They went home to cut, sew, tie, and pray as fast as they could. When word of their work got around at church, they received more requests. They realized there was a need for more prayer quilts than they could make on their own.

The Prayer Quilt Ministry—Prayers & Squares—was born.

Where quilts were sent, the idea took root. People who received them or added prayers to them wanted to bring the ministry to their own churches. In 1996, when Wendy moved to the Community Church of Poway, her new congregation embraced the idea of prayer quilts as a ministry. They became the second chapter of Prayers & Squares. By 1999, there were Prayers & Squares chapters in churches throughout southern California. As quilts were sent farther afield, the ministry grew. By 2000, there were chapters far away from San Diego—in Michigan, Ohio, and Florida.

As this book is written, there are more than 440 Prayers & Squares chapters across the United States and Canada. Chapters have been started overseas, too, in Australia, New Zealand, and the Marshall Islands. One of the newest

*Hope deferred makes the heart sick, but a desire fulfilled is a tree of life.*

PROVERBS 13:12

additions is a congregation in Abu Dhabi in the United Arab Emirates. As the ministry has grown geographically, so has it grown denominationally. Today, there are Prayer Quilt Ministry chapters in Lutheran, United Church of Christ, Presbyterian, Baptist, Seventh-Day Adventist, Assembly of God, Catholic, and numerous non-denominational congregations.

The reasons to give prayer quilts have blossomed, too. While most are made for people in crisis, they are also pieced, stitched, and tied for more joyful occasions. Prayer quilts have been given to babies before their christenings or baptisms and to young people before they are confirmed or graduate from school. Since September 11, 2001, uncounted numbers of "prayer squares," hanky-sized patches of red, white, and blue with four ties, have been made and sent to American troops in Afghanistan and Iraq. Prayer quilters report that the young men and women overseas wear them under their combat helmets or over their hearts.

There are as many stories like Kody's as there have been Prayers & Squares quilts. Unfortunately, Kody's doesn't end as happily as those who knew him, loved him, stitched for him, and prayed for him would have wished. In November 2003, Kody died unexpectedly at the age of 14. His grandmother, one of the original Prayers & Squares quilters, still has his quilt.

But though Kody is gone, the ministry he inspired remains. And its goal to love and comfort people through prayer has remained unchanged since Kody's prayer quilt was spread across his hospital bed. To further that goal, Prayers & Squares needs the nimble fingers and thoughtful prayers of every willing worker, regardless of religious affiliation or ability to manipulate a needle.

But a warning—making prayer quilts can become addictive. It can take your understanding of God, and the way God works in the world, to an entirely

*America is not like a blanket—one piece of unbroken cloth, the same color, the same texture, the same size. America is more like a quilt—many patches, many pieces, many colors, many sizes, all woven and held together by a common thread.*

JESSE JACKSON**

new level. "The quilt is a vehicle for prayer, a vehicle for God's love," says Kathy Cueva, president of the Prayer Quilt Ministry. "Once that happens, once you feel the hand of God touching you and you feel the love of Christ working through you, you will never go back."

*Do all the good you can,*

*By all the means you can,*

*In all the ways you can,*

*In all the places you can,*

*At all the times you can,*

*To all the people you can,*

*As long as ever you can.*

JOHN WESLEY

# CHAPTER THREE
# STITCH ONE, PRAY TOO

## Finding Meaning in the Work

"God speaks in the silence of the heart.
Listening is the beginning of prayer."

—MOTHER TERESA

Time for full disclosure: I am not a quilter. I have dabbled here and there—made the odd patchwork square and even took a class once—though I have never actually completed a quilt. But I am a committed crafter who finds the time to work every single day in some medium, whether knitting, beading, needlepoint, or papercrafts. Working with my hands to create something I consider beautiful is, for me, as necessary as food, sleep, or love. It's something that I simply cannot imagine *not* doing. And when I'm crafting, that's the time I find myself most open and alert to discovering God moving in mystery through my life. When I take up a needle, I feel myself tapping into something divine inside of me.

*Hands are the
heart's landscape.*

Pope John Paul II

*Whatever your
hand finds to do,
do with your might.*

Ecclesiastes 9:10

What is it about crafting that brings me to such a special, sacred aware-ness? I think it's the fact that when I'm crafting I feel most grounded in and connected to my past. When I hold a needle, I'm aware of a line like a thread that runs from me back through the generations to all other women who came before me in the craft. For someone who's moved from place to place most of her life and whose family tree is more like a family stick, this is a very powerful feeling. Practicing traditional crafts like quilting can bring a rootedness in tra-dition—the same thing that many of us find in our religious practices and in our churches. That sense of rootedness is not something easily found in our fast-paced, technology-driven times.

I'm not alone in feeling this way. Untold numbers of crafters, many of them quilters, before me have discovered that there's something about work-ing with the hands that can bring a deeper understanding of God and of our purpose in God's universe. Perhaps it's because when we're making something, we're engaging in an act of creation—an act that we, then, share with God, our Creator. Our creations are extensions of God's creations. And, when we craft, we're using talents, skills, and abilities that came to us from the hand of God. To me, it isn't a stretch to imagine that the use of these abilities can be a link to the Mystery that originally gave them to us. I don't know. And it doesn't mat-ter. All that I know is that when I am crafting I feel more alive and more involved in my inner spiritual life than at any other time.

More people are joining in this discovery. In the past decade, there has been a huge resurgence of interest in the traditional handicrafts: quilting, knit-ting, crocheting, and sewing. At the same time, many people are rethinking what they want from their religious faith. No longer satisfied with just sitting in a house of worship for an hour or so a week, many are seeking a connection to the divine in their daily lives—at work, at home, outdoors, even in the car.

They're seeking what author Sue Bender calls the "everyday sacred"—the ability to turn the most ordinary tasks and experiences into an opportunity for spiritual exploration.[1]

Many people—women and men alike—are finding that the traditional handicrafts lend themselves beautifully to both the practice and expression of faith. There are now religion-based quilting, knitting, and scrapbooking retreats around the country where participants routinely blend prayer, meditation, and worship with their cutting, stitching, and pasting. Colleges and seminaries of every stripe offer courses on religion and crafts. Books on blending the two, books like this one, abound.

Dr. Carolyn Mazloomi is a quilter, quilt historian, and quilt curator at the forefront of the move to recognize and value the spiritual qualities of the craft. She is founder of the Women of Color Quilters Network and one of her quilts is in the collection of the Smithsonian's American Art Museum. To her, it is impossible to quilt without endowing the fabric with her faith in a benign, loving, all-knowing God.

"For me, as an artist, there is no separation between art and religion," Carolyn says. "To me, art is worship because both art and religion deal with man's self-understanding. Both spring forth from the spirit of humanity. There is a godly connection at work. You cannot create unless you are guided by the Spirit. That is the target of the finished product and that is the target of the soul."

For Carolyn, it is no leap of faith to believe that a quilt crafted with prayer and soul is not only made with sacredness, but can also be endowed with the power to heal. "Oh my Lord, yes," she says. "I put so much of myself in the creation of that quilt that it takes on the energy that I put in it, the energy that springs forth from my spirit. I believe it is anointed with God's energy because

*Made by hand, the craft object bears the fingerprints, real or metaphorical, of the person who fashioned it. These fingerprints are not the equivalent of the artist's signature, for they are not a name. Nor are they a mark or a brand. They are a sign: the almost invisible scar commemorating our original brotherhood or sisterhood.*

OCTAVIO PAZ**

that is what is guiding the artist. Through that belief in your creation, the quilt is very powerful."

The act of praying while quilting endows the fabric with a gift and a power, Carolyn says. "When you are working on a quilt, you have a meditative process going on. You have time to talk to God. That is imbued in the quilt. It is. And, too, it serves a purpose, and that purpose is greater than the artist's purpose. The purpose is God's purpose."

Kathy Cueva, president of the Prayer Quilt Ministry, also believes the energy of prayer can be transferred into fabric. Many times, she reports, she's found that a quilt she's working on becomes "almost too hot" to hand stitch. An emergency room nurse, she once attended a conference on alternative medicine when she heard something that helped explain this to her. The presenter "was talking about quantum physics and the energy field created by healing touch," she says. "Some call it karma, some call it quantum physics, but we all have it. We can inject this into a quilt. The quilt then becomes a channel of grace and sacrament because of the spirit entering it."

It isn't only the recipient of the quilt who benefits from the prayers said in its making. In the intensity of the creative spirit, the quilter, too, will find his or her relationship to God tightened with every stitch. "The creation of the work raises the quilter closer to the divine," Carolyn says. "It opens up your heart and lifts you up. . . . I know this is strange to say, but when I am working [on a quilt] I can feel the power of my work, and it is a feeling I can't describe. I know I am in a different place, and my feet aren't planted on the ground because I can feel my spirit soaring."

Tara Jon Manning is another textile artist who knows firsthand the power of craft to express the spirit and touch others. She is a knitter and a Buddhist whose book *Mindful Knitting: Inviting Contemplative Practice to the Craft* dis-

---

*Let the favor of the Lord our God be upon us, and prosper for us the work of our hands—O prosper the work of our hands!*

PSALM 90:17

*Back of every creation, supporting it like an arch, is faith. Enthusiasm is nothing: it comes and goes. But if one believes, then miracles occur.*

HENRY MILLER*

cusses how knitters, or any crafters, can bring a sense of purpose, awareness, and prayerfulness to their work. She, too, believes a handmade item crafted with prayer and intention for another person is invested with a special power. "I really believe that there is an imprint that goes into something that is crafted by hand," Tara explains. "You are holding that thought and that intention in that place. It is imbued in the object. It is the idea and the essence of generosity."

Tara writes that a basic tenet of Buddhism is that we should work to relieve the suffering of others. We can do that when we make a quilt or another handmade item to give to someone in crisis. Such an item and the work it takes to produce it, she says, connects us to all human beings because it "connects us to the understanding that there is suffering world. Suffering is part of what it means to be human. It is one thing all human beings have in common. But they also have the antidote in common, which is love and good will."

Tara also says the impact of such an item can go way beyond the person it is intended to comfort. "I believe that when one chooses to do something positive toward the alleviation of suffering, it multiplies in the world in ways you may not even be aware of," she explains. "Just think about what that teddy bear or that blanket can do for a child on the other side of the world, what a gift can do to change things. Someone may be inspired to do the same thing by seeing your project. That potential is truly inspiring. The teeniest contribution can have magnificent repercussions, and if we can get more people to think that way we can get the world to shift to a more enlightened place."

If a quilt can change the world, think of what it can do for the one small person it is made for. Perhaps she is sick. Perhaps she is alone. Perhaps she is facing great uncertainty and feeling enormous fear. For each of these people, a prayer quilt can be a lifeline, a link to what makes them feel safe and part of

*There is a comfort in the strength of love;*

*'Twill make a thing endurable, which else*

*Would overset the brain, or break the heart.*

WILLIAM WORDSWORTH*

*You give but little when you give of your possessions. It is when you give of yourself that you truly give.*

Kahlil Gibran

a larger family. Carolyn has made many quilts for hospice and AIDS patients and has seen this happen repeatedly. "When you put your soulful energy into a quilt, your prayerful energy, you cannot help but transfer that to the recipient," she says. "And when recipients see that, they will know that you love them, because it was not so easy turning out that work. They will know you took so much time, put so much of yourself into that work, so much of your prayerfulness."

"They will know it is special," she says, beginning to break into tears. "When they feel it, they will know it is special."

The prayer quilters at Foothills United Methodist Church in La Mesa, California, know this, too. When they gathered for a sewing circle, their talk about the power their prayers give the fabric turned mystical. "I don't feel the prayer quilt is just material," says Jo Ann Long. "When I'm making the quilt, I'm thinking that whoever gets this quilt, I want it to guide and protect them. That's an attitude of prayer and I feel that makes the prayer quilt a living thing." Dorothy Dunhouse, another La Mesa prayer quilter, agrees. "The energy of our prayers goes into the minds of the person who receives the prayer quilt," she says. "They get strength and courage and hope. The strength of that, especially of the hope, is very powerful. And if they're not going to survive, our prayers can give them the courage to face that."

So, as you sit to make a prayer quilt, know that you are doing so much more than joining fabric and bits of thread. You are building a link to the past, to the present and to the future: The past is there in quilting's history as a traditional craft; the present is there in your desire to ease another's current situation; and the future is there in the hope you are building into every stitch and every prayer of the quilt.

## STORY OF A QUILT
# *Cynthia's Quilt*

When Cynthia Vereen's prayer quilt was placed in her lap, it placed God in her heart.

Diagnosed with breast cancer, Cynthia was quickly scheduled for surgery, chemotherapy, and radiation. She was scared. But having been raised in an atheist household, she did not turn to God in her distress. Instead, she turned to family and friends in her community of La Mesa, California.

One of those friends was a member of a church where there has been a Prayers & Squares chapter almost since the ministry's start. The friend asked Cynthia if she would be willing to receive a prayer quilt. "I kind of didn't know what that was," Cynthia remembers. "She had to explain it to me and, not having Jesus or God in my life, I thought, well, with my situation I needed all the help I could get."

When the quilt was done—embellished with cats in honor of Cynthia's pets—the friend brought the quilt to Cynthia's home and spread it across her.

That was when something changed.

"It was a confirmation that there really was a God," Cynthia recalls. "It gave me hope and faith because all these people had hope and faith. That told me that there had to be something more. It was the seed being planted."

When her chemo started, Cynthia was more sick than she had ever been in her life. Sometimes it was so bad, she made a bed for herself on the bathroom floor. Her prayer quilt was always nearby. In the worst of it, another friend came to help her through.

"She had her hands on me," Cynthia says. "She would say, 'Just give it to the Lord, just let it go.' And I didn't know what she was talking about. But out of desperation, I said, 'God, I can't take it anymore. I am done. I am yours. Let me just go silently now. I want to die. Just take me, please, God.' I did give myself up."

Then there was a peace, Cynthia says. "There was a release. And it all started clicking."

As soon as she was well enough, Cynthia began attending church. Today, she is a member of Skyline Church in La Mesa. In early 2005, though she didn't know how to quilt, she started a chapter of the Prayer Quilt Ministry there. Her faith in God and her work in the ministry have brought a new direction to her life.

"I kept asking the Lord, how can I be a better servant?" she explains. "How can I use my talents to serve you? And this is it. I am here to serve others. I am a Martha."

A Martha who is cancer-free.

*For this is the message you have heard from the beginning, that we should love one another.*

1 JOHN 3:11

CHAPTER FOUR

# THE THREE COMMANDMENTS

## Rules to Sew By

"Commandments are loving counsel from a wise Father.
Our understanding and concept of God as a loving and
personal Heavenly Father allows us no other definition.
He gives us commandments for one reason only—
because he loves us and wants us to be happy."

—PAUL DUNN, MORMON ELDER AND AUTHOR

Just as there are few rules in praying, there are few rules in the Prayers &
Squares Ministry. Each chapter is free to organize as its members wish, make
what quilts its members like, and tie them in a setting and manner that suits
their congregation best.

But there are three basic rules that every ministry participant, from the
most novice to the most experienced, must consider inviolable. They are the
backbone of the ministry, and without them its purpose and spirit would col-
lapse. They are so important to the integrity of the ministry its founders call
them "The Three Commandments."

## The First Commandment

*This ministry is about praying and not about quilting. Make prayer the purpose of your ministry. Involve as many as people as possible in your prayer efforts and work to promote an active prayer life among participants.*

Without the prayers, this ministry is little more than an outlet for pretty blankets. And while there are certainly people in want of blankets and other basic necessities, the goal of this ministry lies not just in keeping people physically warm, but in keeping them spiritually warm, too. That's not to say that homeless or other needy people in your community aren't worthy of prayer quilts. On the contrary, they're probably among the worthiest. It's only to say that if you create and give a quilt to someone under the banner of this ministry, it must be done with prayer. It is the *prayers* with which the quilts are endowed that speak of God's love. The quilt is only a vehicle for those prayers. With the prayers, the quilt becomes the physical representation of God's love as it is manifested in the congregation that sends that quilt out to someone else. If you cannot accept this commandment, you cannot accept the Prayer Quilt Ministry.

## The Second Commandment

*Before tying a prayer quilt for someone, that person must agree to accept the gift of prayer in the form of a quilt. You must ask the recipient's permission before you give them a prayer quilt. In the case of a child, or of a person who is unable to communicate, a loved one may give permission.*

According to Kathy Cueva, president of the Prayers and Squares Ministry, a prayer quilt is "a channel of grace between the people who pray, the recipient,

*Prayer is not asking. It is a longing of the soul. It is daily admission of one's weakness. . . . It is better in prayer to have a heart without words than words without a heart.*

MOHANDAS K. GANDHI*

and God." For that grace to flow, the person we would give a prayer quilt to must be a willing participant in the prayer quilt's mystery. They must agree to be the object of the prayers of others. The recipient must agree to accept the gift to be true *receivers*, not only of the physical quilt, but also of the prayers of others. Only if the recipient agrees to this can the prayer quilt work. So each prayer quilt must have a sponsor—someone from the congregation or the chapter who takes the responsibility to ask a potential recipient if he or she would be willing to receive a prayer quilt. If the answer is yes, the sponsor explains how the prayer quilt works, asks the recipient what they would have the congregation pray for them, and takes the request back to the chapter.

Linda Befort, a prayer quilter at East Bartlesville Christian Church in Bartlesville, Oklahoma, says she was initially taken aback at the idea of asking someone if they would like to receive prayers. "But then I began to see the wisdom of it," she says. "It's a two-way street. You believe in what God can do for them, and they believe in God and what he can do for them. We're all on the same page." Some people, she says, have turned down the offer of prayers, and therefore, did not receive a prayer quilt.

We also ask permission because in order to open the channel of grace we must know what the recipient would ask us to pray for. For those struggling with illness, physical healing may not be their first wish, and we shouldn't assume that it is. "In the churches I've been in contact with, most of the prayer requests are not for healing," says Carol Neville, a prayer quilter at Community Church of Poway in Poway, California. "More often they're for peace, the ability to accept God's will, or for the [recipient's] family. Sometimes the request is for the doctors or for successful surgery. Sometimes it's pain-free living or the ability to learn to live with a disability, continuous pain, or the loss of a loved one." Recently, Carol's group made a quilt for a healthy five-year-old girl who'd

*Put up at the moment of greatest suffering a prayer, not for thy own escape, but for the enfranchisement of some being dear to thee, and the sovereign spirit will accept thy ransom.*

MARGARET FULLER*

been removed from her home and her drug-using parents and placed her with a foster family—her third. She was understandably feeling disconnected and didn't know where to turn when she was sad and lonely. "The quilt wasn't for healing, but for comfort," explains Carol, "and a reminder that wherever she is, God's love surrounds her."

Prayer is a deeply personal, individual, and usually private form of communication. We honor prayer when we ask permission to give it in the form the person would most like to receive.

And there is another, more practical reason we must ask permission before we give a quilt: We must respect the recipient's privacy. He or she may not want the world to know what it is they are suffering from or struggling with. It's not the business of the Prayer Quilt Ministry to "out" people and their problems.

## The Third Commandment

*Prayer quilts, like prayers, cannot be bought. Never accept payment for a prayer quilt. Those who receive quilts and those who request them must not be obligated to Prayers & Squares in any way.*

Certainly, prayer quilts are "worth" something in terms of money. But their real value lies not in the quality of the materials from which they are made, nor in the intricacy of their designs. Their treasure is in the prayers they represent. How can you attach a monetary value to prayer? Is my prayer worth more than yours? Is a pastor's more valuable than a layperson's? Should a prayer quilt for a cancer victim cost more than one for a premature baby? You simply can't attach a monetary value to something as precious as a prayer quilt. To do so would only cheapen the prayer quilt and devalue your chapter's efforts

*Prayer is the burden of a sigh, The falling of a tear, The upward glancing of an eye When none but God is near.*

JAMES MONTGOMERY[†]

and the ministry's overall contribution to those in crisis. If a prayer quilt is to represent the gift of love people give when they hold others in their thoughts and hearts, then it must also be a true gift—freely given, never bought.

Don't worry about where the money to buy fabric and other ministry needs will come from. As I talked to prayer quilters around the country, I heard as many different ways of making a quilt, of dedicating a quilt, of recording a quilt as there are chapters. But the one thing I heard over and over again, from Michigan to Georgia, from Virginia to California was this: Whenever the bank account was near zero and the fabric closet was near empty, a donation from a recipient or his or her family came in.

These three commandments form the ministry's foundation. If you adhere to them as faithfully as you would their cousins in the Old Testament, the Torah, and the Qur'an, the spirit of the Prayer Quilt Ministry will live and thrive in your chapter and throughout your congregation.

*Love one another with mutual affection; outdo one another in showing honor. Do not lag in zeal, be ardent in spirit, serve the Lord. Rejoice in hope, be patient in suffering, persevere in prayer.*

ROMANS 12:10–12

STORY OF A QUILT

## Mohammed's Quilt

Mohammed was just six years old when he came to the United States for the first time from his home in Saudi Arabia. But this was no happy holiday. Mohammed had bone cancer in his leg, and he was coming to a Houston hospital for surgery that could save it.

At the same time, the Prayers & Squares chapter at East Bartlesville Christian Church in Bartlesville, Oklahoma, had given a prayer quilt to David Willard, a church member in the same Houston hospital for cancer treatment. During the empty and uncertain hours of waiting for tests and treatments, David and his wife, Cindy, struck up a friendship with Mohammed's family. The Willards, who are Christians, and Mohammed's family, who are Muslims, found that while they held different faiths, they had a common belief in the power of God to comfort and heal.

Mohammed's situation quickly grew grim. Doctors found his cancer had spread, requiring more chemotherapy and radiation and postponing surgery. His family was devastated, and their new friends, the Willards, were too. Knowing how much David's prayer quilt had comforted him, Cindy asked the Bartlesville prayer quilters if Mohammed might have a prayer quilt, too.

"We did a lot of praying and decided that God had laid this person here in our lives for a reason," explains Linda Befort, a prayer quilter there. So, following the ministry's second commandment, she wrote to the boy's mother and asked if he would be willing to receive a prayer quilt.

Despite the differences in their beliefs, the answer was, unequivocally, yes. "I believe in the power of God and in His will," the mother wrote back. "Every time I pray, I ask God to heal."

Linda wrote her, "We do not believe that the quilts are magic or have a power in themselves, but we do believe that the one true God we serve has the power to heal, strengthen, and comfort the person to whom the quilt will be given. We believe a quilt is tangible evidence of all the prayers said and represents our faith in God and what he can do." She added that they'd be honored to pray for Mohammed and his family.

Mohammed's prayer quilt was flocked with dozens of tiny images of Curious George. On the back, the prayer quilters wrote several Bible verses they hoped would comfort the family.

Soon after Mohammed received his quilt, doctors were able to put an expandable rod in his leg that would support the cancerous bone and grow with him. He was the youngest person to receive this device in the United States at that time.

Today, Mohammed is back in Saudi Arabia and back in school. His mother keeps in touch with the prayer quilters in Oklahoma. "He is still on crutches, but he is smiling all the time," she wrote. And the prayer quilt is still with him. It is, his mother wrote, "a nice memory from nice people reminding me that there is hope for peace in the world."

*Let us love, not in word or speech, but in truth and action.*

1 JOHN 3:18

# CHAPTER FIVE

# HOW TO MAKE A PRAYER QUILT

## Putting the Pieces Together

"The greatest prayer is patience."

—The Buddha

*It* bears repeating again: This ministry isn't about the quilts. It's about the prayers. Only the prayers. Whether you're embarking on your first prayer quilt or stitching up your hundredth, this phrase should be your mantra every step of the way. Placing the prayers before the quilts is so crucial to the integrity of this ministry that its founders would rather have you add ties and prayers to a store-bought blanket than have you make a prayer quilt so beautiful, perfect, and intricate it could win first prize in a quilt show.

This is good news. Because a prayer quilt can be so simple, it can be tackled by the first-time stitcher or the most experienced sewer. Here are some basic instructions for crafting a prayer quilt.

*We are all patchwork,
and so shapeless and
diverse in composition
that each bit,
each moment,
plays its own game.*

Michel de Montaigne*

## Choosing Fabric

Fabric is less important to a prayer quilt than its prayers. So don't worry too much about choosing fabrics in the right colors with the right tonal values—important in producing art quilts, but not prayer quilts. Just go to a fabric store and let yourself be led. Choose colors and prints you like. Chances are, someone else will like them, too. Whatever fabric you choose, it should be washable. Most prayer quilts are cotton, fleece, or flannel.

Sometimes, fabric will choose you. Members of Prayers & Squares chapters everywhere tell stories of ugly "orphan" fabrics that eventually became beautiful and beloved quilts, as well as stories of "coincidentally" making, say, a pink quilt with horses days before a request for a child's pink horsie quilt comes in. So if you hate bugs, but feel called to make a quilt from fabrics simply crawling with them, go for it. Trust in the Spirit to lead you to the fabric that needs to become a quilt. Ultimately, God will match the right quilt to the right person.

Eventually you will want to have a stash of quilts suitable for a variety of people and requests. You will want more masculine quilts—perhaps in shades of brown, with fabrics that might depict sports, fishing, or the outdoors—as well as feminine quilts in pastels and florals. Children love primary colors and vibrant fabrics with bugs, cartoon figures, tools, and trucks.

You can also make "cheater" prayer quilts. A cheater quilt is made from a fabric panel already printed with a patchwork quilt pattern. It requires little or no piecing. Just add batting, sew it to another piece of fabric, attach ties, say some prayers, and it's a quick prayer quilt. Cheater quilts are particularly useful for new chapters where members need to get some quilts ready for the first requests. And if you are a novice stitcher, they are great projects for practicing your new skills.

Whatever kind of prayer quilt you choose to make, the key is not to over-think it and spend so much time on its construction that someone in need of a prayer quilt goes without. Remember the mantra: It's not about the quilt, it's about the prayers.

## Color and Imagery

There are some colors and quilting patterns that have religious and spiritual significance. Incorporating them into your prayer quilts can give them special meaning.

### Color

*White.* White is the color of innocence, purity, and perfection, and of God as the Creator. In Christianity, it is the color of the Easter and Christmas liturgical seasons. In Buddhism, it represents rest and thinking. In Judaism, white is considered the true color of light.

*Red.* In many religions, red signifies the color of blood. In Christianity, it stands for the blood of Christ and the martyrs, as well as for the fire of Pentecost. In Judaism, this color is associated with strength, joy, and happiness. In Hinduism, red is the color of purity. A Hindu bride dresses for her wedding in fire red.

*Purple.* This is the color of penitence and mourning, of humility and suffering. In Christianity, it is the color of the liturgical seasons of Advent and Lent. In Judaism, purple is associated with purification from sin.

*Green.* The color of nature, hope, renewal, and rebirth, green can symbolize the triumph of life over death. In the Christian calendar, it is the color of

*It is not only prayer that gives God glory but work. Smiting on an anvil, sawing a beam, whitewashing a wall, driving horses, sweeping, scouring, everything gives God some glory if being in his grace you do it as your duty.*

GERARD MANLEY
HOPKINS*

the Trinity and, sometimes, the Epiphany season. In Islam, green is the color of life.

*Black.* This is the color of grief and sorrow.

*Blue.* This is the color of loyalty and steadfastness. In Christianity, it is the shade most associated with the Virgin Mary, whose robes are frequently depicted as robin's egg blue. In Judaism, the Torah commands Jews to dye the border threads of their *tallit*, or prayer shawls, with this color to remind them of the sky and the throne of God. Among Iranians, this is the color of mourning. Some Native Americans consider blue the color of defeat, while others, especially tribes of the Southwest, consider turquoise blue a sacred color.

*Yellow or gold.* These are the colors of the sun, the giver of life. In Buddhism, these colors represent nourishment. In Hinduism, yellow, especially saffron yellow, is sacred and represents fire.

### Quilt symbols

During the eighteenth and nineteenth centuries, American quilters of European descent included many colorful everyday objects in their quilts. To them, these pictures made up a kind of not-so-secret code, as each was intended to convey a specific thought or wish to the recipient of the quilt. African-American quilting is rife with symbols and imagery. Some of these signs and symbols include the heart (love), roses (purity, happiness), the pineapple (hospitality and friendship), the pomegranate (fruitfulness), the diamond (the lifecycle, with four points representing birth, life, death, and rebirth). If you have the skill and the time, or if you find a fabric printed with these symbols, they can convey extra meaning to the prayer quilt.

*Good is a product of the ethical and spiritual artistry of individuals; it cannot be mass-produced.*

ALDOUS HUXLEY*

*Size*

Prayer quilts can be made in any size. For a baby, a 40-inch squares works well for a crib, a stroller, or for wrapping up an infant in someone's arms. For adults, "lap quilts" of 40 to 50 inches wide by 50 to 60 inches long are an accommodating size. They can be laid across a wheelchair or placed on top of a hospital bed and are more portable than a bed-sized quilt.

## Making a Quilt Top

This is the part of the quilt made from small pieces of fabric. It is here you can let your talent and creativity loose. If this is your first quilt, look for simple patterns posted on the Prayers & Squares website (www.prayerquilt.org), or visit other quilting websites to download free patterns or purchase them from designers. There are also any number of good how-to-quilt books available in bookstores or libraries. For beginners, the Rail Fence quilt is a great training ground. It is forgiving of slightly crooked seams and requires only three different fabrics.

Young people say, What is the sense of our small effort? They cannot see that we must lay one brick at at time, take one step at a time; we can be responsible only for the one action in the present moment. But we can beg for an increase of love in our hearts that will vitalize and transform all our individual actions, and know that God will take them and multiply them, as Jesus multiplied the loaves and fishes.

DOROTHY DAY

*When all is said and done, friendship is the only trustworthy fabric of the affections . . . friendship is warmth in cold, firm ground in a bog.*

MILES FRANKLIN\*

### Fabric

For the Rail Fence quilt top, you will need three different pieces of fabric:

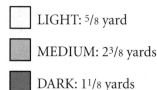

LIGHT: 5/8 yard

MEDIUM: 2 3/8 yards

DARK: 1 1/8 yards

### Cutting out the quilt top

To create the Rail Fence pattern, cut twenty-four strips of fabric, eight of each color, that measure 2 1/2 inches long and run the width of the fabric. These strips will form the center of the quilt top. For the border of the quilt top, cut five strips from the DARK fabric that measure 3 1/2 inches long and run the width of the fabric.

Set aside the remaining MEDIUM fabric for the quilt back.

### Sewing the quilt top

Use one strip of each color fabric to make eight sets of strips. Every strip set should be assembled the same way, with MEDIUM between LIGHT and DARK. One at a time, pin and sew strips wrong sides together, using 1/4 inch seam allowance.

Next, measure the width of your strips across all three colors. This is your "block measurement." It will range between 6 and 6 3/4 inches. If some strips are a little larger or smaller, use the average width (example: 6 1/2 inches).

Cut across each fabric strip to make a block that is the same length as the width of the strip. For example, if the block measurement you took in the previous step was 6½ inches, you will cut your blocks 6½ inches across. Cut out forty-eight square blocks, six from each strip of fabric.

Once you have cut out the blocks, arrange them six blocks across and eight blocks down on a table or bed in the manner shown below. The resulting pattern should resemble a staircase, with the DARK and LIGHT fabric strips forming steps and risers.

Sew the blocks together in rows going across using a ¼ inch seam allowance. When you have eight rows of blocks completed, sew the rows together using a ¼ inch seam allowance.

Life itself is a thread that is never broken, never lost. Do you know why? Because each man makes a knot in the thread during his lifetime: it is the work he has done and that's what gives life to life in the long stretch of time: the usefulness of man on this earth.

JACQUES ROUMAIN*

*Only your compassion
and your loving
kindness are
invincible, and
without limit.*

THICH NHAT HANH

### Attaching the border

Now it is time to frame the blocks. Measure across the quilt top you have just completed. Cut two of the 3¹/2 inch strips of DARK fabric to the same measurement. For example, if your quilt top measures 39 inches across, cut two of the DARK fabric strips to 39 inches. Using a ¹/4 inch seam allowance, pin and sew these two strips to the top and the bottom of the quilt top. Measure the length of the sides of the quilt top, including the two DARK strips just attached, and cut two more DARK strips to the same length. For example, if your quilt top measures 54 inches from top to bottom, cut two 3¹/2 inch DARK strips 54 inches long. Pin and sew these to the sides of the quilt top.

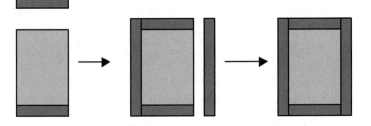

You have now completed a quilt top, ready for batting, backing, and, of course, ties and prayers. Those instructions will be tackled in the next chapter. For now, no matter what pattern you choose, it is important to remember not to get so wrapped up in the quilt top that you never get to the praying. A prayer quilter sews that she may pray, and does not pray that she may sew. As Kathy Cueva says, "too much Martha and not enough Mary" can give us some fabulous and beautiful quilts, but if they never get to their recipients they are not living up to the Prayer Quilt Ministry's goal.

The Rail Fence quilt is only one of many quilt patterns that lend themselves to a relatively quick and easy prayer quilt. There are other suitable patterns available on the Prayer Quilt Ministry's website, www.prayerquilt.org. And if making a whole quilt seems too daunting, the website has instructions for other quilted and tied items invented by members when they had a need that a large prayer quilt could not meet. The most popular of these is the prayer square, a smaller, more portable version of a prayer quilt with a dozen or so ties. There are also patterns for pocket prayer quilts, three-inch tied squares that will fit in a purse or pocket, and a baptismal square that is suitable for a baby. Many chapters are making military prayer squares, small patriotically decorated squares they are shipping to American service men and women overseas. To see examples of these items, and to find out how to start a chapter, visit the Prayer Quilt Ministry's website, www.prayerquilt.org, or write to them at Prayers & Squares International, 3755 Avocado Boulevard, #248, La Mesa, California 91941. To order prayer quilt labels, contact Cornerstone Graphics, P.O. Box 176, Poway, California 92074.

STORY OF A QUILT

## *Hillview Acres Quilts*

Mother's Day is a time when kids are supposed to be with their moms. But what if you are a kid whose mother is dead, or abusive, or just unable to take care of you? What if you've been taken away from your mom and family and placed in a group home? What would your Mother's Day be like?

In early 2005, thoughts like these troubled Peggy Pearson, who lives down the street from the Hillview Acres Christian Home in Chino, California. Hillview Acres is a place for twenty-four of the most troubled of troubled kids, most of whom are victims of domestic violence or sexual abuse, or sometimes both. Peggy had seen these kids walk by her house to and from school outings. She had seen them at Inland Hills Church, where she and some of these young people worshipped on Sundays. She had seen the emptiness in their eyes.

So, as Mother's Day approached, a thought came to her. "God just laid it on my heart," she recalls. Wouldn't prayer quilts help these kids get through what would otherwise be a desolate day? But Mother's Day was only six weeks away. And twenty-four kids meant the Prayers & Squares ministry at Inland Hills would need to make twenty-four quilts—one every day and a half—a huge task for a chapter with two dozen members, not all of them skillful sewers.

But when Peggy asked her fellow Prayers & Squares members if they were willing to tackle this project, not one said no. They took their idea to the children's chaplain at Hillview Acres, and asked him for help with choosing the right colors and patterns for the right children. Once they knew who liked horses, who liked cats, and whose favorite color was pink and whose was purple, the Inland Hills chapter went to work. These quilts were gifts of true community—only one of the twenty-four was made by a single person from start to finish. The rest passed through many hands, with one person cutting, another piecing, another layering, another binding, and another adding the ties. "They went the rounds," says Peggy.

The Thursday before Mother's Day, the quilts were tied, and the women laid them on the children's beds. When the kids returned from their classrooms, the quilts were there to greet them. Now, each child who comes to Hillview Acres receives a quilt from the Inland Hills Prayers & Squares chapter. "How it touched them, touched us," Peggy says. "It was a reminder of how everything is connected."

*Of all duties,*
*prayer certainly*
*is the sweetest*
*and most easy.*

LAURENCE STERNE*

# CHAPTER SIX

# CROSSES AND BORDERS

---

## Finishing a Prayer Quilt

"Do not worry about anything, but in everything by prayer and supplication with thanksgiving let your requests be made known to God. And the peace of God, which passes all understanding, will guard your hearts and your minds in Christ Jesus."

—PHILIPPIANS 4:6–7

*N*ow you have a quilt top. But without the prayers, this is still just a couple of pieces of fabric and some stitching. To make your quilt top into a prayer quilt, you must first layer it and then give it the ties that will hold fast the prayers you, your congregation, and the recipient's friends and families will soon invest it with.

## Assembling the Prayer Quilt

To assemble a prayer quilt, you will need:

- A completed quilt top

- A sewing machine

- A quilt back—fabric cut 1 to 2 inches wider than the quilt top in width and length

- Quilt batting cut to same size as the quilt back

- Coordinating fabric for binding, cut in strips 2$^1$/$_2$ inches wide

- Thread that matches binding fabric

- fifty or more safety pins

- #5 perle cotton floss, two to three skeins (This is a floss that is thicker than embroidery floss. It comes in many different-colored skeins.)

- Crewel needles with eyes large enough for perle cotton

- Masking tape

- Blunt-tipped scissors

- An iron and ironing board

- A Prayers & Squares label, available from the ministry, or make your own

### Layering the quilt

Iron both the quilt top and the quilt back to make them as smooth as possible. Spread out the quilt backing, *wrong-side up*, on a hard table or on the floor. Secure all four edges with masking tape to the table or floor, beginning on one side and moving to its opposite side, pulling slightly taut. Place the batting on

*Is not prayer also a study of truth—a sally of the soul into the unfound infinite? No man ever prayed heartily, without learning something.*

Ralph Waldo Emerson*

top of the quilt backing, smoothing out any wrinkles from the center. Make sure the batting is centered on the quilt back. Lay the quilt top *face up* on the batting and smooth it from the center to the edges. Check that the quilt top is centered and square to the quilt back.

Using the safety pins, pin through all three layers, placing the pins 6 to 8 inches apart. It's a good idea *not* to place the pins where a tie will eventually go so you do not have to manipulate the thread through the quilt's layers at the same time you are trying to avoid hitting the safety pins.

### Sewing top and back together

Remove the masking tape from the edges of the quilt. Your quilt should be so well pinned that all the layers are firmly attached to each other. Using a sewing machine, stitch around the edges of the quilt and through all three layers, about 1/4 inch in from the edge of the quilt top. You may want to use the width of your sewing machine's presser foot as a guide. Using scissors or a rotary cutter, trim any excess batting even with the quilt top.

### Binding

With matching thread, sew as many of the 21/2-inch strips of binding fabric together across their short ends as you need to fit around the outside of the quilt. The binding is like a frame for the rest of the quilt. For example, if you are making a 40-inch-square baby quilt, multiply 40 inches (the length of one side) by 4 (the number of sides) to get 160 inches, the total length of the binding. Don't forget to allow for seams— about 1/4 of an inch at both ends of every piece of the binding. When you've sewn the binding strips together into one long piece, fold it in half lengthwise, *wrong sides together*, and press. Sew this to the back of the quilt, keeping the raw edges of the binding even with the

*Do your best to present yourself to God as one approved by him, a worker who has no need to be ashamed, rightly explaining the word of truth.*

2 Timothy 2:15

raw edges of the quilt (figure 1). Use a $1/4$-inch seam and mitre the corners (figure 2). Bring the binding to the front so the folded edge just covers the seam line and sew with a zig-zag or a straight stitch close to the fold (figure 3).

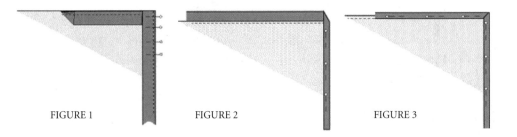

FIGURE 1            FIGURE 2            FIGURE 3

### Preparing the ties

Each prayer quilt should be held together with eighty to one hundred ties. The ties are important not only to hold all three layers together through washings and use, but also to provide enough places for people to anchor their prayers. You may use more than one hundred ties, but try not to use less than eighty. These quilts are both well-loved and well-used, going from home to hospital, sickbed to washing machine many, many times, so make sure your quilt is strong enough to take a lot of loving. (You can also do very basic machine quilting in a simple design to stabilize the quilt, but this is not necessary).

Cut the perle cotton into lengths about 3 feet long. Thread the crewel needle and bring both thread ends together and move the needle to the center of the cotton. Now you have a doubled thread about 18 inches long. Decide where you want your ties—they should be between 4 and 8 inches apart. (Your quilt top may give you "clues" to where the ties will work best. If the design is made

*Blest be the tie that binds*

*Our hearts in Christian love;*

*The fellowship of kindred minds*

*Is like to that above.*

JOHN FAWCETT,
EIGHTEENTH-CENTURY
HYMN-WRITER

of small pieced squares, you might want to put ties in some of the corners where the squares meet. If it is made of larger pieced blocks, you might want to put the ties at the four corners of the blocks.)

Working from the top layer to the bottom, pierce all three layers of fabric with the threaded needle. Come back up and out the top about 1/4 of an inch from where you started. If your stitches are bigger than 1/4 of an inch, the ties will pucker the quilt top. Cut the thread, leaving tails about 3 or 4 inches long for people to tie.

### Labeling

Labeling every prayer quilt is crucial. It will not only help you keep track of how many quilts you've distributed, as well as the dates and recipients, but it also adds a personal touch to each quilt, which the recipient cannot fail to notice.

Official Prayers & Squares labels are available from the ministry's website, www.prayerquilt.org. But if you run out of pre-printed labels with the official logo, just handwrite the necessary information on a piece of muslin with a permanent marker. The following wording will do just fine:

> This prayer quilt was made for
> *(name)*
> with love, hope, and prayers.
> Each knot represents a prayer that was said for you.
> *(month, year)*
>
> Prayers & Squares, The Prayer Quilt Ministry
> *(church or organization's name)*
> *(city, state)*

*The ties between gentle folk are as pure as water.*

CHINESE PROVERB*

When all the ties have been placed, remove the safety pins and hand sew a Prayers & Squares label on one of the lower corners of the quilt back.

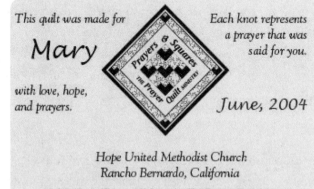

*This quilt was made for* **Mary** *with love, hope, and prayers.*

*Each knot represents a prayer that was said for you.*

*June, 2004*

Hope United Methodist Church
Rancho Bernardo, California

*A Member of Prayers & Squares, The Prayer Quilt Ministry*

Lastly, use a safety pin to attach a tag with washing instructions to every quilt. If you wish, you can include your church or organization's contact information on this tag. Many prayer quilt recipients will want to call or write you to thank you for your gift.

> Your prayer quilt may be machine washed with cold water and mild detergent, and line dried or dried on low heat to reduce wear and fading. DO NOT IRON. Any loose knots should be tightened before washing to prevent them from coming out. Even if the knot comes out, the PRAYER LASTS FOREVER.

*The wish to pray is a prayer in itself. . . . God can ask no more than that of us.*

GEORGES BERNANOS*

## Record Keeping

Your chapter may start with just a trickle of requests for prayer quilts, but soon you will be inundated as people see how much the quilts come to mean to those in need. You'll need to keep a record of the quilts you give away. It is a good idea to number your quilts with both the year and the quilt number. So the fifth quilt given away in 2005 would appear as "05-5" in the record book. You can then use this number to identify everything else related to this quilt—photos, request forms, thank-you notes, and so on. When the quilt is finally presented to the recipient, be sure to record the date it was given and to whom and where it was delivered or sent.

You may keep your records as you see fit. Some chapters keep theirs in a computer file, others make line-by-line entries in a journal. For others, records are more like family scrapbooks, with photos of the quilts, detailed descriptions of their pattern and construction, and thank-you notes from recipients

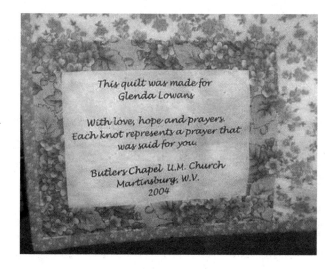

This quilt was made for
Glenda Lowans

With love, hope and prayers.
Each knot represents a prayer that
was said for you

Butlers Chapel U.M. Church
Martinsburg, W.V.
2004

*Everybody can be great . . . because anybody can serve. You don't have to have a college degree to serve. You don't have to make your subject and verb agree to serve. You only need a heart full of grace. A soul generated by love.*

MARTIN LUTHER
KING JR.

and their families. The more illustrative the record book, the more people will want to flip through it to see the pretty quilts and read about the ways they affected the people they were given to. Left on the table where prayer quilts are being tied, a well-tended journal or scrapbook can attract support to your chapter and its ministry.

## Cross Words

Once when making a prayer quilt, Wendy Mathson ran out of fabric. She needed a creative and eye-pleasing way to "stretch" the material she was using for the back of the quilt.

Wendy likes to make prayer quilts that are between 46 and 50 inches wide—big enough for the recipients to wrap around themselves to ward off the chill of a hospital or the loneliness of the sickroom. But most fabric comes in widths of between 40 and 44 inches—just shy of what's needed to form a quilt back from a single piece of fabric. So Wendy decided to cut the fabric for the quilt back in half, right down the middle, top to bottom, and add a second piece of coordinating fabric in a long, vertical strip. From there, it was only one more step to cut again in the opposite, horizontal direction and sew in a second strip to form a cross. She says the cross on the back is a "silent testimony" of her faith.

To make a cross on the back of your quilt, you will need two pieces of fabric: a piece of fabric that will form the quilt's backing and a contrasting piece of fabric that will form the cross.

For the cross, first measure the width of your quilt top. Then measure the width of the contrasting cross fabric, excluding the selvages. Subtract the width of the contrasting fabric from the width of the quilt top.

*Let us love our God supremely, Let us love each other, too.*

GEORGE ATKIN,
NINETEENTH-CENTURY
HYMN-WRITER[2]

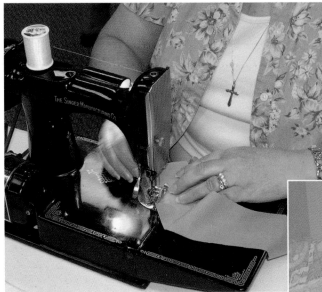

For example, if your quilt top is 50 inches wide and your contrasting fabric is 42 inches (the average width of cotton fabric, minus the selvages) your measurement would be 8 inches. Then, add 3¹/₂ inches to this number to allow for seams. So, 8 inches plus 3¹/₂ inches equals 11¹/₂ inches.

Cut three strips of cross fabric 11¹/₂ inches wide, cutting from selvage edge to selvage edge.

Next, measure the length of your quilt top and subtract the width of your cross strips. For example, if your quilt is 80 inches long and the width of your cross strips is 11¹/₂ inches, your measurement would be 68¹/₂ inches. Again, add 3¹/₂ inches for seams. The answer—72 inches in our example—is the length of the piece of background fabric you will need.

Cut the background fabric across its width to make two sections (figure 1). You do not need to measure, but can if you would like to. One of the cut pieces should be about twice the size of the other.

Pin one of the cross strips between the two pieces of background fabric and sew. Cut the three joined pieces in half vertically (figure 2).

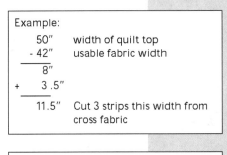

```
Example:
      50"      width of quilt top
   - 42"       usable fabric width
   ──────
      8"
 +   3 .5"
   ──────
     11.5"     Cut 3 strips this width from
               cross fabric
```

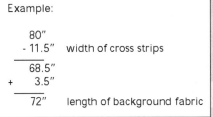

```
Example:
      80"
   - 11.5"     width of cross strips
   ──────
     68.5"
 +    3.5"
   ──────
      72"      length of background fabric
```

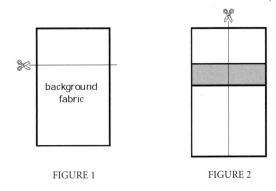

FIGURE 1          FIGURE 2

*The more we come out and do good to others, the more our hearts will be purified, and God will be in them.*

SRI SWAMI VIVEKANANDA, HINDU MYSTIC

*Faith: You can do very little with it, but you can do nothing without it.*

SAMUEL BUTLER\*

You should have two strips of cross fabric left. Sew these together along their shorter sides to make one long strip. Sew this strip to the already assembled pieces of background and cross fabric, centering it and lining up the strip's center seam with the lower seams of the first two pieces (figure 3).

Trim edges if you need to. The result should look like a cross (figure 4).

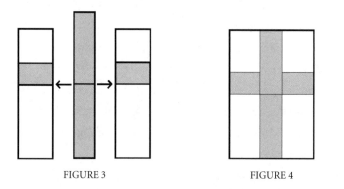

FIGURE 3          FIGURE 4

Adding a fabric cross to the back of a prayer quilt is not a requirement of the Prayer Quilt Ministry. It's up to the individual Prayers & Squares chapters to decide whether placing a fabric cross on the back of their prayer quilts is right for their ministry, their church, and, most importantly, the recipients of their quilts. "The cross is a symbol that means something to many of us," Wendy explains. "But quite a few of our quilts go to people who do not profess a particular faith or belief system. Many believe in God but are not sure about Jesus, the resurrection, and the symbolism of the cross."

"Remember," Wendy cautions, "our membership and our recipient list is not limited to Christian groups. It's open to anyone who believes in the power of prayer."

So what to do? To cross or not to cross? Members of some Prayers & Squares chapters say to exclude the crosses from their quilts would be unthinkable. To them, the cross on the back of their prayer quilts has become an integral part of the ministry, a literal sign that they are working and praying in Christ's name.

At New Community Church of Vista in Vista, California, Kay Bouris says her chapter always puts crosses on the backs of its quilts because the cross "is a symbol of our faith and the loving sacrifice our Lord made for each one of us." Members of her chapter feel the fabric cross shows their love and concern for those who are suffering, and that it points "to the source of all goodness, our Lord Jesus Christ." The fabric cross is also a reminder to everyone who comes in contact with the quilt, from its construction through its giving away, that the Prayer Quilt Ministry is about something much more important than the craft of quilting. "All this work should glorify Jesus and not the individuals who are making the quilts," Kay says. "The cross is a reminder to the giver and receiver that Jesus is the one who heals, comforts, and restores us."

The prayer quilters at East Bartlesville Christian Church in Bartlesville, Oklahoma, put crosses on the backs of their quilts if they have enough fabric to do so. But they also write one or more Bible verses on the backs in indelible ink. "I couldn't give away that first quilt without God's word on it," says Linda Befort, a prayer quilter there. "I want God's word to lay right there on that person."

Members of other Prayers & Squares chapters say they don't put crosses on the backs of their prayer quilts, but their reasons are varied. Some refrain out of respect for the beliefs of others who may not share the Christian faith, while some omit the cross for more practical reasons.

*Taking the first footstep with a good thought, the second with a good word, and the third with a good deed, I entered paradise.*

ZOROASTER

*Faith is the highest passion in a human being. Many in every generation may not come that far, but none comes further.*

SÖREN KIERKEGAARD*

Lorna Barrowman says sewers in her chapter at Palisades United Methodist Church in Capistrano Beach, California, have never put crosses on the backs of their quilts. At first, this was out of practical considerations—when Lorna started her church's chapter, she was the only participant, and didn't have time to piece the backs of quilts as well as the fronts. But now, she and the other stitchers leave the crosses off out of concern for others' beliefs.

Before beginning chemotherapy treatment for breast cancer, Cynthia Vereen received a prayer quilt without a cross on the back. But, her quilt means no less to her for that lack. "I know that if my quilt had a cross on the back I would have been very humbled and would have felt even more love from strangers," she says. "But just because there isn't a cross on the back of my quilt doesn't make it any less special." Today, her chapter at Skyline Church in La Mesa, California, doesn't add crosses because the majority of them are too inexperienced as quilters and sewers. Cynthia says, "It's not at all that we don't honor our Lord and Savior, it's just keeping up with demand."

The Prayers & Squares chapter at Brighton First United Methodist Church in Brighton, Michigan, has found its own answer to the question. Their quilters use only one pattern for their prayer quilts, a kaleidoscope that moves outward from four triangular pieces placed point to point in the center. Not only does the center look like a cross, but its three-sided pieces can be taken to represent the Trinity of Father, Son, and Holy Spirit. This pattern resonates with the Brighton quilters' Christian beliefs. "Since the cross is centered, it symbolizes that Christ is central to our lives," explains Carol Riffe, a member there. "It symbolizes the love, hope, and faith that we believe in and that we hope the prayer quilts bring to the recipients." The group attaches a tag to each quilt that explains the meaning of the quilt's triangles and how its colors of light and dark represent the good and bad times of our lives. But they make a point of not emphasizing the cross pattern and allowing recipients to draw their own meaning from the quilt.

Whether you or your chapter sews crosses onto the backs of your quilts is up to you. As Kathy Cueva says, "Do as you feel led." The most important thing is not to let their inclusion become a requirement of your faith, or the faith of the recipient. "We don't want our ministry to be used to tell people what to believe," Wendy Mathson says. "If they believe something different than we do, that's just fine with us—so long as they believe that their prayers are heard and answered."

*Productive work, love and thought are possible only if a person can be, when necessary, quiet and alone. To be able to listen to oneself is the necessary condition for relating oneself to others.*

ERICH FROMM,
GERMAN-AMERICAN
PSYCHOLOGIST

# CHAPTER SEVEN

# THE TIES THAT BIND US

## Tying a Prayer Quilt

"When he entered the house, the blind men came
to him; and Jesus said to them, 'Do you believe that I am
able to do this?' They said to him, 'Yes, Lord.' Then he
touched their eyes and said, 'According to your faith
let it be done to you.' And their eyes were opened."

—MATTHEW 9:28–30

I first heard about the Prayer Quilt Ministry during a telephone interview with Kathy Cueva, the ministry's president, for an article I was writing about crafting as a spiritual practice. She told me how the quilts are tied, and that as they are tied prayers are said and that they believe those prayers are literally bound into the fabric of the quilt.

That's really nice, I thought. How sweet.

I didn't really get it.

Then, when I began working on this book, I attended a church service where five quilts were presented and then laid out in the vestry for tying and prayers. Among the first people to approach the quilts were an elderly man and a small girl—grandfather and grand-daughter, no doubt. The man, dressed in his Sunday best suit, took the girl's soft little hands in his own gnarled ones and placed them together on the ties of the first quilt. He bent his head down to her and said, "See? Like this," as he wrapped the thread right over left, left over right. "Now pray with me," he said. They bowed their heads together, his gray and white one a few inches above the gold and amber of hers.

I got it.

Just as it is the ties that hold the prayer quilt together, it is the prayers uttered when they are tied that bind the quilt's givers to its recipient. These ties join us, not just as a community of faith, but also as a community of human beings. The ties, then, are more than cotton thread. They are the bond between all people—the link between all children of God.

When you tie a knot, you use your hands. Because of this, I like to think that the act of tying the knots is symbolic of the laying on of hands, a tradition of Christian healing that goes back to the ministry of Jesus. The Gospels recount more than forty instances of Jesus' healing miracles, showing a healing touch that could cure everything from leprosy to blindness and raise the dead. Belief in this kind of healing touch is found among many contemporary Christians, from Roman Catholics to Southern Baptists, who place their hands upon those who are ill and pray they be blessed or healed. Though my hands do not bring physical healing, I do believe my touch, like the touch of any compassionate person, can comfort the sick and the scared. So when I tie a prayer quilt and place my hands on the fabric and the ties, I imagine that I'm also laying my hands on the person who will receive the quilt. In this way, I'm not only

*Man is a knot, a web, a mesh into which relationships are tied. Only those relationships matter.*

Antoine de Saint-Exupéry, French poet*

reaching out to the recipient with prayer, but also with my belief that God wants us to love and care for one another. To me, this makes the ties the most important part of the Prayer Quilt Ministry.

Because the ties are so special, they should be made in an atmosphere that is worthy of all they represent. When you tie a prayer quilt, the surroundings should be prayerful and meditative. Some chapters play music when they tie quilts; others tie them in silence. Some read communal prayers aloud before they tie quilts, others lift only the prayers in their hearts as they make the ties.

Some congregations make prayer quilts a regular part of Sunday services, spreading them out on the communion rail to add color and cheeriness to their worship time. In others, quilts remain in the vestry, or other area outside the sanctuary, and a worship leader asks those gathered to stop and say a prayer and make a tie when the service is over.

Ministry members at some churches set up one or two tables and spread the quilts out upon them. Beside each quilt they place a sign that explains who the quilt is for and what prayers its recipient or family members have requested. Some chapters print small cards for parishioners to take home, so quilt recipients can be remembered in prayers throughout the week. Many churches also display a sign that shows how to make a square knot.

Some churches have come up with original ways of making the prayer quilts a part of the congregation's routine. In Apopka, Florida, members of Forest Lake Seventh-Day Adventist Church lay out quilts for tying in the foyer before the service. They invite recipients and their families to attend the service and call them forward to be blessed and prayed for by the pastor and the congregation. As the pastor and the congregation pray, the recipients and their families add their knots and prayers to the quilt. When the quilts are tied by the congregation, ministry members place a framed picture of the recipient on

*Silence is the element in which great things fashion themselves.*

MAURICE MAETERLINCK*

top of the quilt, next to the prayer request. "The picture adds a lot," says Jo Ann Roth, a prayer quilter there. "People like to see who they are praying for. It gives a mental image to carry with them as they continue to pray during the days ahead."

However you tie your quilts, let it be with the intention of creating a sacred space where prayer and reflection will thrive. If you're tying quilts in the vestry, narthex, or other busy area of your church, you may want to have a small cassette tape or compact disc player nearby to play hymns or other worship music. You may want to have one or two small candles lit nearby. Flowers, too, add an element of grace.

There is no right or wrong way to tie a prayer quilt. While a knot can come untied, the prayers it holds fast cannot be unsaid. But there is a best way to tie a prayer quilt—in a square knot, right over left, then left over right. Such knots

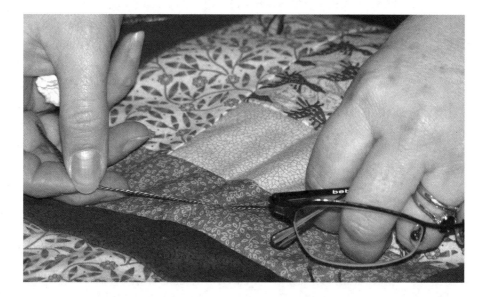

*The value of persistent prayer is not that he will hear us . . . but that we will finally hear him.*

WILLIAM McGILL**

are sturdy and will withstand many washings and worried fingerings by the recipient. After the quilt has been tied, trim all the tied threads to about 1 1/2 inches long.

You may want to leave some threads untied for family members, friends, and even doctors and nurses to tie after the quilt is given. Again, the power of the prayer quilt is only amplified when people beyond the congregation—people who may be of different faiths, or no particular faith—join in praying for and supporting the recipient.

Once a prayer quilt has been dedicated and tied, it will be given to the recipient and begin its work of comfort and care. Ministry members hope the recipient will come through the crisis and the prayer quilt can then adorn a corner of a couch or the arm of a chair. But it is not uncommon for prayer quilt recipients to have another crisis, especially if they're struggling with cancer or some other chronic illness. In this case, another prayer quilt isn't necessary. The first quilt, with all its original ties—and original prayers—can be rededicated and retied. Such quilts are even more powerful in their ability to comfort as they have been reinforced, in a way, with another round of good thoughts and wishes.

❧

Regard your servant's prayer and his plea, O Lord my God,
heeding the cry and the prayer that your servant prays to you today;
that your eyes may be open night and day toward this house,
the place of which you said, 'My name shall be there,' that you may
heed the prayer that your servant prays toward this place.
—1 Kings 8:28–29

*Help us to respond*
*as we go from this place*
*so that we become vessels*
*of healing and grace.*
Martie McMane*

STORY OF A QUILT

## Myron's Quilt

As an associate pastor at Point Loma Presbyterian Church, Brad Gustafson was used to seeing an array of colorful prayer quilts. He was used to bowing his head for their recipients and tying knots with their colorful threads. He didn't think he would ever need one.

Then his father, Myron, developed an illness that baffled the doctors. He was tested for many things, but no treatment seemed to help. "We thought we were losing him," Brad recalls.

Hearing of his father's condition, Prayer Quilt Ministry members at his church, in San Diego, California, asked if they could make a prayer quilt and send it to Brad's father in Aurora, Nebraska. After checking with his mom and dad, Brad said sure.

The next Sunday, a blue, white, and yellow quilt was among several placed before the congregation, awaiting prayers. As Brad introduced the quilts—something he did almost every week—his voice broke. "I said, 'This is for my dad who is experiencing some health issues and we are not sure what is going on. I would very much appreciate your prayers.'" They were given as the knots were tied—for strength, for healing, for peace.

Days later, Brad and his wife flew to Nebraska to be with his dad. The first thing he saw in his parents' house was his father under the quilt. It caught him off guard. "The world shrank," Brad says. "Suddenly the distance just evaporated between these two worlds. This world of my church in San Diego was right there in the living room where my father was touch-and-go with his own health. Suddenly for me, the two were almost one."

The bond intensified when friends stopped to visit Brad's father and asked about the quilt. Told its ties held the prayers of people far away, they asked if they too could add their prayers and a knot to the quilt. "It was very powerful to pray together and to place whatever was going to happen next not only into the doctor's hands but into God's hands," Brad says.

Ultimately, Myron recovered and was the guest of honor at his own eightieth birthday party. Talking about his illness with his son, Brad's father wondered why everyone had been so worried about him. "My dad said he hadn't felt close to death," Brad says. "It was as if he had been carried through the experience without too much anxiety."

"I do not point to the prayer quilt and say that was the magic carpet," Brad continues. "But it was an incredible comfort to this minister 1,500 miles away from my congregation."

The prayer quilt now sits on the back of the sofa in the Gustafsons' living room in Aurora. "It is there as a reminder not only of that harrowing experience of being face-to-face with my father's mortality," Brad explains, "but also that all of these prayers surrounded my father and the rest of us at that terrible time."

*Silence alone is respectable and respected. I believe God to be silence.*

Henry Brooks Adams*

# CHAPTER EIGHT
# CONTEMPLATIVE QUILTING
## Inviting God into the Process

"There come times when I have nothing more to tell God.
If I were to continue to pray in words, I would have to repeat
what I have already said. At such times it is wonderful to
say to God, 'May I be in Thy presence, Lord? I have nothing
more to say to Thee, but I do love to be in Thy presence.'"

—OLE HALLESBY, NORWEGIAN MINISTER[3]

As many of us know from experience, combining the craft of quilting
with the practice of praying can be powerful and transforming. The stillness
and solitude of the creative process can take us to a place where prayer can
spring forth and fly up freely and frequently. In such a place, the quilter can
climb to a new level in his or her relationship with God.

*But this is not to suggest that praying while you're quilting is a requirement of
the Prayer Quilt Ministry. It is only required that you pray while you tie the knots.*
But should you want to strengthen your spiritual practice and prayer life, quilting, or doing any other craft, can be a unique opportunity to do so.

This is something I've learned firsthand. When I began working on this book, I figured I had better make a prayer quilt. I wanted my first one to be worthy of the person who would receive it, so I was going to pray really hard. I thought if I gave myself over to the meditative state induced by the hum of the machine and the blur of the fabric, I could pray in time with needle's quick motion. Such a prayer quilt, I thought, would be bursting with prayers, good intentions, and positive thoughts for its eventual owner.

I got some fabric and a simple pattern and sat down at my sewing machine. I thought it would be easy. I can cut a straight line, I can sew a straight seam, and I can certainly pray. But *what* was I going to pray? I didn't know who would eventually get my quilt, so how could I pray for what they would want? I decided I would pray for something very general and something that God, who knows all our needs, would understand. So as I worked, I kept repeating in my head, "Dear God, let this person be at peace. Let this person feel your love."

Yet as I sat there, the violet and rose fabric coursing past my needle, I found the praying wasn't as easy as I thought it would be. I got what the Buddhists call "monkey brain" as my thoughts leapt from peace and love to one inconsequential thing after another: "What will I make for dinner? What is the dog up to? Is my butt too big?" Not at all what I wanted to seep into the cloth!

I lifted my foot from the pedal, stood up, and walked around the room. I didn't want negative or mundane thoughts to be embedded in this prayer quilt. How could I pray more effectively?

I started asking prayer quilters what they do when they make a prayer quilt. How do they make the hours they spend quilting a time of contemplation and prayer? I found that many had developed their own techniques.

Across the country, prayer quilters spoke to me of focusing their minds

*Silence is the general consecration of the universe. Silence is the invisible laying on of the Divine Pontiff's hands upon the world. Silence is at once the most harmless and the most awful thing in all nature. It speaks of the Reserved Forces of Fate. Silence is the only Voice of our God.*

HERMAN MELVILLE*

not on specific things, like what they want for the eventual owner of the prayer quilt, but very generally on God. They simply sat and sewed and contemplated God and God's Mystery. "There's no absolute attitude to be in while you are sewing," Kathy Cueva says. "I am usually just open to where the Spirit leads. I've had a lot of Holy Spirit time when I'm working on quilts. Sometimes I think God talks to me because I'm finally still."

Kathy suggested a "less intentional" attitude. Stop working so hard to send prayers and thoughts out, she advised, and spend more energy on "just listening."

That was a eureka moment for me. What Kathy had done was give me permission to tap into the ancient Christian tradition of contemplative prayer.

## Contemplative Prayer

Contemplative prayer is best understood by looking at its Latin root, *contemplare*, which means "in the temple." It's a way of being open to the divine by listening instead of speaking or doing. In the words of Thomas Keating, a Trappist monk who helped revive this ancient spiritual practice, "Contemplative prayer is the opening of mind and heart—our whole being—to God, the Ultimate Mystery, beyond thoughts, words and emotions. We open our awareness to God whom we know by faith is within us, closer than breathing, closer than thinking, closer than choosing—closer than consciousness itself. Contemplative prayer is a process of interior purification leading, if we consent, to divine union."[4] That's what I wanted—a way to know God's presence while I quilted.

There are a variety of ways to practice contemplative prayer and many of them can be practiced at the same time as quilting, or engaging in any other

*These things God has revealed to us through the Spirit; for the Spirit searches everything, even the depths of God. For what human being knows what is truly human except the human spirit that is within?*

1 CORINTHIANS 2:10–11

craft or activity. And because contemplation of the divine has been a part of the spiritual practice of peoples of every faith, the practice lends itself beautifully to the goal of the Prayer Quilt Ministry to include people of all traditions.

So, before I sat back down at my sewing machine, I began investigating what type of contemplative prayer practice would work best for me. Because I was familiar with some of the works of Keating, I decided I would give centering prayer a try.

### Centering Prayer

Centering prayer is a contemplative practice that dates back to the Desert Fathers and Mothers, first- and second-century Christians who made their homes in the deserts of the Middle East and devoted themselves to lives of prayer. Today, it is used by Christians and non-Christians alike to still busy thoughts and open the mind to God. Centering prayer comes about through quiet, stillness, a certain kind of breathing, and the repetition of a single, special word, spoken or unspoken.

Teachers of centering prayer suggest that we choose a sacred word to repeat over and over again, like a mantra in Eastern religious practices. The word can be inherently religious, like *God, Jesus, Abba, Father, Mother, Mary,* or *Amen.* Or, it can be more generally spiritual, such as *love, peace, mercy, listen, silence, stillness, faith, trust,* or *yes.* Choose a word that speaks most clearly to you and to your intention to welcome God into your work in the Prayer Quilt Ministry, as well as into your heart.

As you sit at your sewing machine, think of your chosen sacred word and focus your inner attention on it. Don't concentrate so much on the word's definition, but rather on the word as a symbol of your desire to bring God into the process of what you're doing—making a prayer quilt.

*It is only with the heart that one can see rightly; what is essential is invisible to the eye.*

ANTOINE DE SAINT-EXUPERY, FRENCH POET

When I went back to my prayer quilt, I chose the word *Abba*, which is Greek and Aramaic for *father*. In some translations of the Gospel of Mark, Jesus addresses God as *Abba Father* in the Garden of Gethsemene, the night before his crucifixion (14:36). How fitting then it seemed to me, to choose this utterance for my prayer quilt as the person who will receive it is likely to confront a personal Gethsemene. To me the word Abba indicated the very essence of God—mercy, understanding, love, and acceptance—qualities I felt sure people of other faiths would also recognize and yearn for from God. So breathing in, breathing out, and repeating *Abba* again and again in my head, I found myself becoming very peaceful, very content. I felt quiet, in the sense that I was untroubled and assured. That feeling, I am sure, made its way into the prayer quilt.

### The Jesus Prayer

In the Gospel of Luke, Jesus tells a parable of a tax collector who beats his breast before God, saying, "God, be merciful to me, a sinner." Eastern Orthodox Christians have adapted this into a meditative prayer they know as "The Jesus Prayer," or the "Prayer of the Heart." On an intake of breath, they say or think "Lord Jesus Christ," and on the release of breathe they think or say, "Have mercy on me, a sinner." After many initial repetitions, the prayer may be reduced to simply "Jesus" on the inhale and "mercy" on the exhale. Orthodox teachers through the ages have considered the Jesus Prayer a portal to a meditative state, a place where random thoughts are stilled and the mind is open to God.

I tried the Jesus Prayer as I was quilting. For me, it wasn't as effective as the centering prayer had been. Perhaps this is because in my faith tradition there is not as much emphasis on sin and repentance as there is in others. I had a great

*Faith is believing what you do not see; the reward of faith is to see what you believe.*

St. Augustine*

deal of difficulty making a deep connection to the word "sinner." If the Jesus Prayer makes a meaningful connection with you, try praying it as you quilt. Match your breath to the prayer, and see where it takes you. Surely, its call for mercy is something everyone touched by the Prayer Quilt Ministry can use, from the cutter and stitcher, whose time is precious, to the recipient, whose health and welfare may be at risk.

### A sacred space

Tara Jon Manning, the Buddhist knitter and author, reports that when she sits down to knit, especially for others, she does something to make the place in which she knits a sacred space. Sometimes she lights a candle or a bit of incense or says a small prayer or blessing. This comes from the ritual practices many Buddhists perform when they enter a temple or other worship space, drawing a boundary between the sacred and the secular. "That brings your attention to what you are doing in that space, right there right now," she says. "It shifts the energy in the space."

This idea speaks to my Methodist roots, where every Sunday morning worship service began with an acolyte lighting the candles on the altar. When I was lucky enough to get a turn, I took the task very seriously. When the flame touched the candlewick and rose high, I felt it marked the beginning of something special, something holy, something quite apart from the rest of my week. Likewise, extinguishing the candles at the end of the service, marked the return to the "everyday." For me, lighting a candle before I begin to work on a prayer quilt is a way to make the everyday sacred. Now, whenever I embark on a session with a prayer quilt, I light a small votive I keep on a table—away from the fabric, of course.

*The relationship to one's fellow man is the relationship of prayer, the relationship to oneself is the relationship of striving; it is from prayer that one draws the strength for one's striving.*

FRANZ KAFKA*

At the end of a session spent knitting for someone else, Tara performs a "dedication of merit" ceremony. From the Shambhala tradition of Tibetan Buddhism this is a small prayer said at the completion of a spiritual practice. There are several variations on the dedication of merit, but Tara's goes, in part, like this:

> By this merit, may all obtain omniscience
> May it defeat the enemy, wrongdoing
> From the Stormy waves of birth, old age,
>    sickness, and death
> From the ocean of samsara, may I free all beings[5]

"I am saying, 'may what I just experienced benefit the world at large,'" Tara says. "Somehow the essence of what I have done or have learned is not just for me, it is for the betterment of the world."

How perfectly this matches the Prayer Quilt Ministry's intentions, I thought. I wrote it down on a piece of paper and laid it by my votive. When I recite it just before blowing out my candle, I feel as if I've further marked my sewing time as special and sacred.

### Sewing prayers

Lynda Ryerson, a prayer quilter in Duluth, Georgia, wanted to make sure her time at the sewing machine was a prayerful time. Like me, she found maintaining a prayerful mindset for a long period a bit of a challenge. So she did some searching on the Internet and found a few prayers for healing that, with a little tweaking of a word here and there, were easily adapted to quilting. I

*When the spirit brings light into our minds, it dispels darkness. We see it, as we do that of the sun at noon, and need not the twilight of reason to show it us.*

JOHN LOCKE*

have included those prayers in chapter eleven. Now, when she sits down to make prayer quilts as part of the Prayers & Squares chapter at Duluth First United Methodist Church, she reads one of these prayers either aloud or silently. Only then does she sit down to work on a prayer quilt. She says marking her quilting time with a prayer keeps her focused on the ministry's mission. "Otherwise, I would forget the purpose of what I am making," she explains. Combining praying and quilting has brought her a new understanding of prayer's meaning and how it works. "A lot of people look at prayer as a way to get what they want. But prayer is really a way to talk to God. Prayer, to me, plants the seed in the soil for God's answer, not ours."

Lynda was kind enough to make copies of her prayers and share them with other Duluth prayer quilters. I brought one of these copies home with me. The next time I took out the sewing machine and lit my votive, I said one of Lynda's prayers. Its impact on me was immediate. I felt that I was asking God for all that is good and possible for a total stranger. Then, as I sat down to sew, I felt as if the very essence of my prayers were passing into the fabric with the thrusts of the needle. I was confident that when I finished this quilt it would be as full of my prayers as it could possibly be.

Not every method will work for everyone—nor should it, as our individual prayers should never adapt themselves to a cookie-cutter mold, but should be as unique as our souls. So do what works best for you. Just keep looking for a place, both physical and spiritual, where your prayers can bubble up from the still, quiet center of your being. That is the place where quilts, and all other forms of creative crafts, are conceived of and dreamed about. That is the place where God listens and speaks.

*In the deserts
of the heart*

*Let the healing
fountain start,*

*In the prison
of his days*

*Teach the free man
how to praise.*

W. H. Auden*

## STORY OF A QUILT
# *John's Quilt*

Debbie Torian is a member of Inland Hills Community Church in Chino, California, and her husband, John, was the recipient of a quilt.

"My husband had come home from the hospital," she recalls, "after being in intensive care for a week. He was tired and weak, but I urged him to go to church with me that morning. After the service, we went to the Prayers & Squares table to pray over the quilts waiting for the prayer ties. When he saw the one with his name on it, he started crying." He needed the quilt almost immediately, when, a couple of days later he was back in the hospital again. He draped the prayer quilt across his chest each night when he went to sleep.

He would come in and out of consciousness for a few hours at a time, but was unable to speak much. The nurses, concerned about contaminants in the room, asked Debbie to take the quilt home and wash it. When she brought it back again, freshly laundered, during one of his more coherent times, his eyes lit up. "I was wondering where that had gone," he said. "I wanted it with me." Touching it and knowing people were praying for him gave him comfort through the long, scary nights.

"I didn't realize until then how very much it meant to him," Debbie recalls, "nor that he was aware it was missing. He went to heaven a few days later. It now lays across his pillow on our bed, continuing the mission of healing and soothing for me."

# CHAPTER NINE

# THE DARK SIDE

## Does God Hear Our Prayers?

"Prayers do not die. . . . The lips that utter them may close
in death, or the heart that felt them may cease to beat,
but the prayer lives before God, and God's heart is set on them.
Prayers outlive the lives of those who utter them—
outlive a generation, outlive an age, outlive a world."

—E. M. BOUNDS[6]

When I visit a Prayers & Squares chapter, I always ask to see their scrapbooks. I love to look at the riot of colors made by all those prayer quilts and to read the thank-you notes from recipients and their families. You cannot help but be touched in some way by their troubled journey. The pain, uncertainty, and fear felt by a prayer quilt recipient comes through in their prayer requests, thank-you notes, and, all too often, their obituaries.

Flipping through the pages of one scrapbook, I was brought up short by how many recipients did not get well again. On one page, a child of two succumbed to cancer. On another, a mother of three died in a car accident. On a third, a man with a brain tumor was taken from his wife only a year into their marriage. It went on and on. This is the dark side of the Prayer Quilt Ministry—the side where the bright fabric colors may dim and the softness of the batting may be blunted. It is the place where babies die and good people suffer.

Certainly, as I read, there were good outcomes as well. Still, my heart was weighed down by all the sadness, all the pain, all the heartache in those pages. How, I wondered, do prayer quilters cope with so much sorrow and disappointment? How do they find the patience to design yet another quilt, to cut out all those small fabric scraps and put in all those tiny ties? How do they find the inspiration to pray over and over again for good, positive outcomes for what can often seem an unending string of bad situations?

How hard it must be, I thought, for those in the Prayer Quilt Ministry to see so many sick brothers and sisters fail to pull through; how discouraging to see them die. How painful it must be to see so many of their prayers go unanswered.

I was wrong. People in the Prayer Quilt Ministry have learned and absorbed something I have not. They know that God is not a jukebox; you don't just plunk in a quarter and dance to the tune you want. They have explored firsthand one of the great enigmas about God that people of every faith have long struggled with: Why does God let bad things happen? And what they have learned, and I had not, is that the most basic lesson of prayer is that it cannot be fully understood. Prayer, the language between God and his creations, is a central mystery of faith and one that we will never be able to truly comprehend. "I know there is a bigger plan that I will probably never understand," says Lynda Ryerson of Duluth First United Methodist Church in Duluth, Georgia. "That is what faith is. I have learned to ask what good is God

*Illness is the night-side of life, a more onerous citizenship. Everyone who is born holds dual citizenship, in the kingdom of the well and in the kingdom of the sick. Although we all prefer to use only the good passport, sooner or later each of us is obliged, at least for a spell, to identify ourselves as citizens of that other place.*

SUSAN SONTAG*

going to bring out of this situation. There is sorrow, yes. But I have a peace about it. You have to believe that good is going to come out of every situation, even the bad ones."

And there *is* good in every bad situation, prayer quilters say. The key is to find it. True, we may pray that a person be healed, and we may mean we want them to be physically healed. But the kind of healing the person needs, and may ultimately get, is not ours to determine. Through their work in the Prayer Quilt Ministry, prayer quilters have accepted that the final outcome of any situation is in God's hands, not theirs. "We see God answering prayers when . . . a small child lays a hand on a tie and prays for their friend who comes to church with them a few weeks later," says Carol Neville, a prayer quilter in Poway, California. "We see God answering prayers when, after the recipient dies, their family member finds comfort and peace in church or alone with God." From so much suffering, Carol draws a personal lesson of faith. "Maybe bad things happen because we grow from them," she says. "Why so many bad things come to people who don't deserve it, we are not meant to know. But just as shaking a young tree helps its roots to grow and become a taller, stronger, healthier tree, so do we become strengthened by 'being shaken.' And our families and friends can grow from the experience as well. As long as we ask God to help us through."

Christine Abbott, a prayer quilter at Inland Hills Community Church in Chino, California, says she sees God's answers to her prayers in the solace he brings to the recipients and their families. "Maybe the recipients make it, but if they don't, I receive some comfort knowing that they could touch a physical representation of prayer," she says. "Jesus didn't always fix people's problems completely, and neither do we, but if we can play a part in joy for them, I am lifted up."

*The miracles of the church seem to me to rest not so much upon faces or voices or healing power coming suddenly near to us from afar off, but upon our perceptions being made finer, so that for a moment our eyes can see and our ears can hear what is there about us always.*

WILLA CATHER*

*An act of love,*
*a voluntary taking*
*on oneself of some*
*of the pain of the*
*world, increases*
*the courage and love*
*and hope of all.*

DOROTHY DAY

"I try not to fret over these questions because if I do I am not showing God respect," says Cynthia Vereen, a prayer quilter at Skyline Church in La Mesa, California, and a recipient of a prayer quilt during a battle with breast cancer. "Only he has the power, and I just have to put my complete trust in him. I pray, pray, pray for those who are suffering. I pray for our Lord and Savior to hear our prayers, but mainly I ask that He gives each person comfort, because in reality I know that no matter what ails them I know that God will heal them, if not here on earth, then in heaven."

Often, it isn't only the prayer quilt recipient who is "healed" by a prayer quilt. Prayer quilters, too, say accompanying the recipients through their tough times can bring a new perspective to their own lives. "Sometimes it takes seeing a loved one suffer to realize how precious good health and normal lives are and how temporary our lives on this earth are," said Peggy Pearson, another Inland Hills Community Church prayer quilter. "Sometimes it takes seeing a believer suffer with grace to know how important having God in our life is. . . . God has a plan for everyone, and we just need to trust Him and know that He has a specific purpose for each and every event in our lives."

Still, many prayer quilters say seeing so much suffering is not easy. But, as Betsy Wegner, a prayer quilter at Riverlakes Community Church in Bakersfield, California, says, each prayer quilter has a choice to make. You can either hide away from the darkness, or you can open your mind and your heart to it and learn from it. "Sometimes it can be very depressing," she says. "But it is like doing hospice work. You have to go into it with your eyes open and focus on the positive." Witnessing the pain and suffering of others can become a lesson in understanding how God works and moves in all of our lives, she continues. It can become a window into understanding why he allows pain and suffering and bad things to come into the lives of good people.

Nancy Davidson, a member of Brighton First United Methodist Church in Brighton, Michigan, was the perfect window into that. In 1997, she was given a blue, purple, and pink quilt to see her through her debilitating migraines. When she was later diagnosed with advanced breast cancer that had spread to her brain and her bones, she kept her quilt close. On one of the last Sundays of her life, she came to Brighton leaning on a walker to tie knots and add her prayers to someone else's prayer quilt. "I pray for other people every day," she said at the time. "We all need help."

Kathy Cueva, the Prayer Quilt Ministry's president, always looks for the light in the darkness. Sometimes, she literally sees it. Once, while delivering a prayer quilt to a sixteen-year-old girl hospitalized with extensive head and neck cancer, she stopped to talk with the girl's mother. They cried and hugged. Kathy laid the quilt on the girl's still body, and turned to go. It was then that she noticed a bright light filling the room. She stopped, making sure her eyes were not playing tricks on her, not blinded by tears or bleary from too much stitching. "I left filled with knowing that the young girl, who had lived long beyond all predictions, was surrounded by the Holy Spirit. I am always alert for the awesomeness of God in the presence of a prayer quilt."

*The steadfast love of the Lord never ceases, his mercies never come to an end; they are new every morning; great is your faithfulness. "The Lord is my portion," says my soul, "therefore I will hope in him."*

Lamentations 3:22–24

# CHAPTER TEN
# MANY HANDS MAKE LIGHT WORK

## Beyond the "Church Ladies"

*"I was ever in the habit of working with my hands,
and it is my firm wish that all other brethren work also."*

—St. Francis of Assisi

Whathat does it mean to be a "member" of the Prayer Quilt Ministry? What do we mean when we say we "belong" to a Prayers & Squares chapter?

There are no membership cards, no membership dues. No embarrassing initiation rituals; not even a secret handshake. You don't even have to quilt, sew, or come anywhere near a needle and thread. All you have to do to be a member in good standing of the Prayer Quilt Ministry is to pray.

So everyone—literally, *everyone*—from the smallest child to the oldest adult has something they can contribute to the ministry. And because so many different people can be involved, the Prayer Quilt Ministry can bring a deep sense of unity and pride to a congregation as well as strength to its sense of mission and purpose within the broader community. "I believe we have become more conscious of our prayer life and our connection to one another in the body of Christ," says Lisa Bruget-Cass, pastor of Wesley United Methodist Church in Worcester, Massachusetts, home to Prayers & Squares chapter number 142. "When one suffers, we all suffer. When one rejoices, we all rejoice. People know that when they go through a difficult time, they have a community that will tangibly reach out in service and in prayer." And Tommy Simpson, pastor of Tates Creek Christian Church in Lexington, Kentucky, says the Prayer Quilt Ministry brings his congregation a sense of perspective. "We have learned that there are more important things to be concerned about rather than the trivial matters, which seem to gridlock churches," he says. "Not that we are immune to trivial matters, but praying for the needs of people greatly helps to keep us focused. Praying for each other is one of the reasons for which we exist. The prayer quilts help to keep that in front of us."

The key to unlocking the riches of the Prayers & Squares ministry is drawing members from beyond the usual circle of "church ladies." There are enough jobs that need to be done to get and keep a Prayers & Squares chapter up and running that there should be something for everyone in your congregation—men, boys, teenagers, and children included. Here are some ideas for getting those who do not quilt involved.

## Behind the Scenes Jobs

*Fabric organization.* The fabric gathered by and donated to the ministry needs to be kept in order by colors and fabric types (cotton, flannel, fleece, and so on). It can be sorted, folded, and stacked in whatever container suits your

*It is in the shelter
of each other
that the people live.*

IRISH PROVERB

group best—a closet, a bin, a set of shelves. It's also helpful to attach a tag to the pieces of fabric with information crucial to the making of a quilt, like its length and width and fiber content.

*Fabric cutting.* Not everyone likes to sew, but some people still like the feel of fabric between their fingers. Using a pattern, fabric cutters can cut out all the pieces for a quilt top and place them in gallon-sized zipper bags with pattern instructions. These bags can be kept ready for sewers to make into a quilt.

*Pressing.* When quilts are sewn together, they often require the seam allowances between pieces be pressed to one side or the other of the seam. Anyone who can iron a handkerchief can serve as a presser. "We have one man who isn't too well who loves to do our ironing for us," says Nancy Fuss, a prayer quilter at East Valley Church of the Nazarene in Apache Junction, Arizona. "Two other ladies who have a hard time seeing come and help iron, too." One or more pressers are usually on hand for group sewing sessions and may bring their own iron and board from home, if necessary.

*Attaching ties.* This is a crucial part of the ministry and a wonderful role for people whose eyesight or agility may make other tasks too difficult. One or more "tyers" can be present at group sewing sessions, or completed quilts can be taken to their homes. This job can be quite prayerful and spiritually rewarding.

*Making labels, hearts, or crosses.* Every Prayers & Squares quilt has a ministry label attached on the back. Some chapters also personalize their labels by embroidering hearts or crosses on them. Some include a drawing of an angel. Others write inspiring Bible verses—maybe even the recipient's favorite—on

*Prayers go up and blessings come down.*

YIDDISH PROVERB

*I don't do great things. I do small things with great love.*

MOTHER TERESA

the label with an indelible marker. None of this is required, but adding one of these touches to your ministry can bring in people who do not sew or quilt. Look for someone known for their beautiful handwriting or their memory of Bible verses.

*Sewing machine maintenance.* Sewing machines should be oiled at least once a month, and many people like to oil theirs more frequently. This is a great place to get men or teenagers involved. Ask them to come to group sewing sessions and bring some sewing machine oil and a few necessary tools, especially a set of screwdrivers.

## Public Relations Needs

*Contact person.* There should be one or two members of your chapter who will be the "go to" persons for those requesting quilts. They should be readily available by telephone and e-mail and should respond quickly to requests because some of them will be emergency situations. The contact person should get as much information about the recipient as possible—age, gender, illness or crisis, job, hobbies, likes and dislikes. This will aid the quilt chooser in selecting just the right prayer quilt.

*Quilt chooser.* This person receives quilt requests from the contact person (though in some chapters, the contact person and the quilt chooser are one and the same). Based on the information received from the contact person, they select an appropriate prayer quilt from the chapter's set of completed quilts.

*Table attendants.* Quilts laid out for tying by the congregation should be attended by one or two people. These attendants should set up tables, spread

*Have you had a kindness shown? Pass it on; 'Twas not given for thee alone, Pass it on; Let it travel down the years, Let it wipe another's tears, Till in Heaven the deed appears, Pass it on.*

HENRY BURTON

out the prayer quilts, and display signs with the recipients' specific prayer requests. They can direct people to any ties that remain untied and can answer questions about the ministry.

*Delivery.* After the quilts are tied, they need to be delivered to their recipients. Helpers are needed to bring the quilts to the recipients' homes or hospital rooms, or to box the quilts and have them shipped to their destination. Anyone with a car or easy access to public transportation can perform this duty in the ministry.

## Ministry Maintenance

*Word processor.* This person can be responsible for printing the signs that go on the tables beside the quilts that are being tied on a given day. The signs should include the recipients' names and their specific prayer requests. Some chapters also print up small business cards with the same information for those who tie the quilts to take home so they may remember the recipients in their later prayers.

*Photographer.* Every quilt should be photographed before it is given away or before it is tied. In addition, displaying photos of the quilts as they are presented to and tied by the congregation can help instill a sense of belonging to the ministry throughout the church body. Look for someone skilled in digital photography—perhaps a teenager on the yearbook staff or in the photography club of their school.

*Scrapbooker and record keeper.* Every prayer quilt needs to be recorded. You will want to keep track of its number in your chapter's history, who it went to, and

*Giving connects two people, the giver and the receiver, and this connection gives birth to a new sense of belonging.*

Deepak Chopra

*I expect to pass through this world but once, therefore any good that I can do, or any kindness that I can show to any fellow creature, let me do it now; let me not defer it or neglect it, for I shall not come this way again.*

Stephen Grellett

what it looked like. Many chapters keep this information in a scrapbook, with pictures of the quilts, pictures of the recipients (when available), and thank-you notes. This is a role in which teenagers can excel.

*Refreshments.* No one does anything well on an empty stomach. Try enlisting non-quilters to bring snacks and beverages to group sewing sessions or other gatherings. Then gently suggest they pick up an iron, a skein of perle cotton and, eventually, a needle and thread.

Including as many people as possible in the work of the Prayer Quilt Ministry will give your congregation a sense of ownership about its work; the more people involved in the making, tying, and giving away, the deeper the roots of this ministry will grow into the participants' hearts and minds. If you can accomplish that, the ministry's mission to comfort, love, and encourage in the name of God will reach into the next generation and beyond.

*We are, each of us angels with only one wing; and we can only fly by embracing one another.*

LUCIANO DE CRESCENZO,
ITALIAN FILMMAKER

*Thousands of candles can be lighted from a single candle, and the life of the candle will not be shortened.*

THE BUDDHA

CHAPTER ELEVEN

# QUILTING PRAYERS

## Words for the
## Prayer Quilt Ministry

"Pray in the Spirit at all times in every prayer
and supplication. To that end keep alert and
always persevere in supplication for all the saints."

—EPHESIANS 6:18

*W*hile the fabrics may be beautiful and the stitches that bind them may
be even and tight, it is the prayers—our minds and hearts lifted to God on
behalf of others—that make a prayer quilt an instrument of grace. The prayer
quilt is a tool. Only God is the healer.

From the purchase of the fabric to the delivery of the quilt, there are innu-
merable opportunities to pray. There are no requirements for when you pray
or what you pray—only that you must pray. Do as you and your group feel led.
Before you step into the fabric store or open your fabric closet, you may want
to say a small prayer asking God to guide you to the right material for the
quilt's recipient. If you wish to start group sewing sessions by joining hands in

prayer, go for it. If you want to bow your head alone before your sewing machine, that's fine, too. Just pray. Then pray some more. The more you pray, the more power the quilt will have to comfort and to heal.

These are some prayers gathered and written by members of the Prayer Quilt Ministry. Feel free to use them as you see fit.

*Ask, and it will be given you; search, and you will find; knock, and the door will be opened for you. For everyone that asks, receives, and everyone who searches finds, and for everyone who knocks, the door will be opened.*

MATTHEW 7:7–8

## Prayers for Sewing Alone

*These prayers are good for those times when you are alone at home in front of your sewing machine, just about to begin work on a planned quilt or are seeking inspiration as you begin a quilt. They came from Lynda Ryerson of Duluth First United Methodist Church in Duluth, Georgia.*

*A*lmighty *Father,* this person is in need of special miracles. I pray that the Spirit of God will perform them. Father, I believe that the power of God will go into this quilt to do the work that God intended and promised. It will be done in Jesus' name.

Father, in Jesus' name I lay my hands on this quilt and claim that your healing, miracle working, and delivering power goes into it as this quilt is put on the sick person willing to receive it. All this I ask in Christ's holy name.

I thank you, Lord, because I am allowed to ask for God's healing power. I continue to believe in your miracle of healing as I work on this quilt. My prayer is that the person who receives this quilt will feel your almighty power raging through his body to a cure. Let him be healed in Jesus' name.

Father, I know your steadfast love endures. As I work on this quilt, I ask that you answer the prayers of the person who believes in you. As our father who has compassion on his children, I pray you may reveal your complete love to this person whose needs you already know. In your son's holy name, I pray.

*For truly I tell you, if you have faith the size of a mustard seed, you will say to this mountain, "Move from here to there," and it will remove; and nothing will be impossible for you.*

MATTHEW 17:20

*For we walk by faith, not by sight.*

2 CORINTHIANS 5:7

*Faith moves mountains, but you have to keep pushing while you're praying.*

MASON COOLEY*

*The words of kindness are more healing to a drooping heart than balm or honey.*

SARAH FIELDING*

*Dear God,* as I enter this workplace,
I bring Your presence with me.
I speak Your peace, Your grace, and Your perfect order into the
    atmosphere of this room.
I acknowledge Your Lordship over all that will be spoken, thought,
    decided, and accomplished within these walls.


*Dear Lord, I thank You* for the gifts You have
    deposited in me.
I do not take them lightly, but commit to using them responsibly
    and well.
Give me a fresh supply of truth and beauty; on which to draw
    as I create.

Anoint my creativity, my ideas, my energy so that even my smallest
    task may bring You honor.
Lord, when I am confused, guide me. When I am weary, energize me.
Lord, when I am burned out, infuse me with the light of Your Holy
    Spirit.

May the work that I do and the way I do it, bring hope, life,
    and courage to all that I come in contact with today.
And Oh Lord, even in this day's most stressful moments,
    may I rest in You.
Amen.

## Prayers for Sewing Together

*These prayers can be said by an individual or within a group of quilters. They are taken from a worship service held at Brighton First United Methodist Church in Brighton, Michigan, and were partly inspired by a prayer from Debbie Salter Goodwin's book,* Quilted with Love.

*God of infinite tenderness* and strong compassion, weave your will into the fabric of our lives. Weave your joy into our songs, your peace into our prayers, and your justice into our deeds. Let this time of worship be a holy moment where the frayed edges of our lives are woven into a beautiful tapestry that comforts and blesses, inspires and renews. God of infinite tenderness and strong compassion, weave your love into our service of praise. Amen.

*Creative God,* weaver of the fabric of life, we thank you for its texture and beauty, its versatility and durability. We sometimes fashion our lives into forms that do not please you and that fit us badly. The fabric is pulled and torn and made ugly through our own misuse. Fill us with a skillful and energetic faith that enables us to receive the portions of life we are given and to sew them together according to the pattern of your will. Amen.

*Do not abandon yourselves to despair. We are the Easter people and hallelujah is our song.*

Pope John Paul II

*Be not lax in celebrating.*

*Be not lazy in the festive service of God.*

*Be ablaze with enthusiasm.*

*Let us be an alive, burning offering before the altar of God.*

Hildegard of Bingen, Christian mystic

*Take the pieces of our lives* and stitch them together according to your will. May we yield to the pricks of your needle so that your stitches may surround us with the pattern of your love. May we allow you to order the squares in any way you want, to pattern us by your design so that all will know you quilted us.

*Members of Prayers & Squares at St. Matthew's Episcopal Church in Parker, Colorado, open their meetings with the following prayer.*

*Lord, we thank you* for this work you have given us to do together. We pray you give us the grace to persevere in it and through it to serve you and those who are hurting. Comfort and strengthen those who receive these quilts. All honor and glory is yours in Jesus name.

*The Lord is good to those who wait for him, to the soul that seeks him.*

LAMENTATIONS 3:25

*At Good Shepherd Episcopal Church in Cedar Hill, Texas, members say the following prayer to open their meetings.*

𝒟*ear* ℒ*ord, we thank thee* for this day to come together for the purpose of bringing hope and comfort by making quilts for those that are very ill, facing treatment or surgery. May our faith in your healing help to strengthen them to face whatever comes to pass in their lives. Continue to bless and use us to do thy will that we may be a blessing to others. Keep us strong and uplifted so that we may have words of encouragement for those in need. This we ask in Jesus' name. Amen.

## Prayers for the Dedication and Rededication of Quilts

*The members of St. Mary's Parish in Milford, Michigan, have a special prayer they say before tying a quilt. They fill in the blank with the recipient's name.*

𝒴*ou promise,* 𝒪 𝒢*od,* Giver of all Life
That wherever we go
You will be with us. May we never forget your comforting care
And may our growing faith be a sign to _____
That you will never stop loving us.

*Whatever you ask for in prayer with faith, you will receive.*

Matthew 21:22

*This prayer can be used in a worship service during the dedication of one or more quilts before they are placed before a congregation to be tied or retied. It, too, came from Brighton First United Methodist Church.*

We give thanks, creator God, for those who gather to wash, press, cut, and sew. Bless them as they gather in a community of love to create a tangible sign of our prayers and your grace.

**Praise be to God.**

We give thanks, loving God, for the creativity and care, love and hope that is sewn into each and every quilt. Bless those who answer your call to show mercy and kindness to those in need.

**Praise be to God.**

We give thanks, guiding God, for the lessons of these quilts. Help us to see the beauty in the variety of colors and patterns and to forgive the imperfections just as you see the beauty in each of us and accept and forgive our imperfections.

**Praise be to God.**

Patient God, remind us that our prayers and your love never die. Renew the prayers of these quilts that they may continue to bring comfort and peace to those who have received them and their loved ones.

**Hear us, O God.**

Everlasting God, remind us that you are with those who cry out to you. Remind those who need healing, comfort, rest, courage, strength, patience, renewal, and hope that they are covered not in only these quilts, but in the quilt of your eternal love.

**Hear us, O God.**

*The human community is like the community of birds to a bird, singing to each other. Love is one of the reasons we are singing to one another, love of language itself, love of sound, love of singing itself, and love of the other birds.*

SHARON OLDS*

Restorer God, send your Spirit to fill us, renew us, and energize us for the days ahead. Allow us to be clothed with spirits of light, love, and truth and to go forth from this place to continue our work and share your love with others.

Amen.

## Prayers for the Presentation of Quilts

*Members of St. Mary's Parish's Prayers & Squares chapter recite one of these two prayers when a sponsor gives a prayer quilt to its recipient.*

*May you feel His presence*
Experience His peace
Draw from His strength
Rest in His love
May God bless you and keep you in His loving care.

*Dear Lord, Walk with us today* and grant that we may
Follow in Your footsteps wherever they may lead.
Talk with us today and let us know your gentle counsel in everything
    we think, do, or say.
Be our strength today when we weaken, our courage when we fear, and
    whenever night falls helps us to know that we rest in your Sacred
    Heart.
Amen.

*Those who are kind to the needy honor him.*

PROVERBS 14:31

*He who sows courtesy reaps friendship, and he who plants kindness gathers love.*

ST. BASIL, FOURTH CENTURY CATHOLIC BISHOP

## A Concert of Prayer

*Palisades United Methodist Church in Capistrano Beach, California, marked its first anniversary in the Prayer Quilt Ministry by inviting their prayer quilt recipients and their families to a special worship service. Everyone was given a piece of fabric that would be used in future prayer quilts. During the service, a worship leader asked everyone to hold these pieces of cloth as she led them in the following prayer, composed by church member and prayer quilter Jill Yamada.*

Please take out your fabric piece as we pray.

*Our loving God,* we enter into this time of prayer especially remembering the prayer quilt recipients.

In our longing to do something for our brothers and sisters, Lord, it causes us to search within and discover what you desire of us. You call us to pray for one another and so we do with grateful hearts. We ask for your mercy, your healing touch, your comfort. As it was with the women who just wanted to touch the hem of your garment Lord, so do we. To reach out in our time of need, crying out. Our hope is in you, Lord. We continue to pray for the needs of these individuals, O God, as we lift each one to your throne of grace.

After each name is read, we will continue in silent prayer.

The leader will say "Lord, in Your Mercy," then we will respond collectively "Hear our prayer."

*(Names of prayer quilt recipients are read by a worship leader.)*

Thank you for being among us, Almighty God. For listening to the petitions of your people. We feel your presence, and your abiding peace through the power of the Holy Spirit.

---

*I believe that God prays in us and through us, whether we are praying or not (and whether we believe in God or not). So, any prayer on my part is a conscious response to what God is already doing in my life.*

Malcolm Boyd**

## A Liturgy for the Prayer Quilt Recipient

*The following liturgy is used by the Prayers & Squares chapter at University Lutheran Church in East Lansing, Michigan. They say it when they deliver a quilt to someone, filling the blanks with his or her first name, and presenting them with a printed copy along with the quilt. It was developed by the church's senior pastor, Rev. Fred Fritz. "There is something extra special that happens when we actually wrap them in the quilt," says Bobbie Davis, a member there who has participated in this liturgy. "The power of the Holy Spirit is at work."*

*In the name of* **the Father, and the Son and of the Holy Spirit. Amen.**

A reading from Hebrews 12:1–3:

Therefore, since we are surrounded by so great a cloud of witnesses, let us also lay aside every weight and the sin that clings so closely, and let us run with perseverance the race that is set before us, looking to Jesus the pioneer and perfecter of our faith, who for the sake of the joy that was set before him endured the cross, disregarding its shame, and has taken his seat at the right hand of the throne of God. Consider him who endured such hostility against himself from sinners, so that you may not grow weary or lose heart.

*The human spirit will endure sickness; but a broken spirit— who can bear?*

PROVERBS 18:14

A reading from Philippians 1:3–6:

I thank my God every time I remember you, constantly praying with joy in every one of my prayers for all of you, because of your sharing in the gospel from the first day until now. I am confident of this, that the one who began a good work among you will bring it to completion by the day of Jesus Christ.

_____, receive this quilt as an expression of love and support by your brothers and sisters in Christ at _____. [Church Name] When you wrap yourself in this quilt, may you be warmed and wrapped in prayer.

Let us pray:

**Gracious God, source of all healing and comfort, we give you thanks for your gifts of strength and life, and especially for the gift of your son, Jesus Christ. Enfold _____ in your loving embrace and grant her comfort, healing, and peace.**

The Peace of the Lord be with you.

**And also with you.**

*Faith no doubt moves mountains, but not necessarily to where we want them.*

Mason Cooley*

## A Prayer for the Prayer Quilt Ministry

*After the quilts have been tied and sent and the last scraps of fabric and thread have been swept away, this is a good prayer to say "thank you." It was written by Louise Lucas, a quilter at Point Loma Community Presbyterian Church in San Diego, California, and appears on the Prayers & Squares website.*

### The Quilter's Prayer

Lord, we are humbled by our riches.

We thank you for the gift of the Prayer Quilt Ministry; for those who conceived it and those who saw its worth; for those who continue to support it and those who will join it in your time.

We thank you for the quiltmakers, for the prayer teams, for the donors, and for the staff and clergy of our churches.

Thank you for the technology that allows us to communicate with each other and to travel safely to this gathering.

Thank you for this place that could receive us and hold us. Thank you for the many hands and hearts working to feed us, teach us, and inspire us.

Those of us who make quilts thank you for the forbearance of our families; for the children who make do without our attention and the spouses who chip in with other chores.

Thank you, God, for cotton in all its sturdy softness. Thank you for batting, for thread, for embroidery floss, and for making these materials plentiful for us.

Thank you for color and for the emotion it conveys, from cooling blues to warming yellows to passionate reds.

*God looks unjust but is not. God asks more from those who more is given. They are not greater or better; they have greater responsibility. They must give more service. Live to serve.*

DOM HELDER CAMARA,
CATHOLIC MYSTIC

Thank you for the abilities you give us so that we can imagine and design, and arrange and rearrange these bits of color; so that we can stitch them together into outward and visible signs of your grace, and tie them into our petitions and prayers.

Lord, thank you for the loving people who request our quilts. They see a need and meet it. They follow through for loved ones and, often, strangers. They are the ones who get our quilts into the hands of those who need them.

Most of all, we thank you for the recipients who open themselves up and let us into their lives. By letting us help in our small way, they increase our understanding of your marvelous ways. We remember those recipients who have gone on to your glory, especially those for who the quilts may not have arrived in time, although the prayers always did.

Finally, God, we remember and lift up to you our brothers and sisters throughout the world who do not have quilts for warmth and comfort. We pray that they will know your loving kindness in other ways.

All this we pray in the name of our treasured redeemer, Jesus Christ.

Amen.

*Comfort, comfort
ye my people,
speak ye peace,
thus saith our God;*

*comfort those who
sit in darkness
mourning 'neath
their sorrows' load.*

JOHANN G. OLEARIUS*

CHAPTER TWELVE

# QUILTING FROM THE HEART

## Other Groups that Make Quilts with a Purpose

"Prayer is not an old woman's idle amusement.
Properly understood and applied,
it is the most potent instrument of action."

—MOHANDAS GHANDI

*How does God's love abide in anyone who has the world's goods and sees a brother or sister in need and yet refuses to help?*

1 JOHN 3:17

By no means is the Prayer Quilt Ministry the only group that makes quilts for those in need. Nor is it the only religion-oriented quilting ministry. There are many other quilt and blanket charities with chapters and stitchers across the United States and around the world. If the need for prayer quilts in your community slows down, or if you simply feel moved to make quilts for another cause, you may want to stitch for one of the well-known and well-organized groups listed below.

*Compassion means that if I see my friend and my enemy in equal need, I shall help them both equally. Justice demands that we seek and find the stranger, the broken, the prisoner and comfort them and offer them our help. Here lies the holy compassion of God that causes the devils much distress.*

MECHTILD OF
MAGDEBURG, MEDIEVAL
CATHOLIC MYSTIC

But keep in mind that any quilts you make for other organizations cannot be prayer quilts because they cannot meet the Prayers & Squares commandment that their recipients agree to receive it. A quilt donated to any of these charities should not be put before the congregation to be tied with specific prayers. Still, there is no reason a quilt made for any of these charitable groups cannot be pieced and stitched with your own individual prayers for healing, strength, love, and wholeness.

Some organizations that distribute donated quilts have been left off the list below because they request donations from the recipients. This could violate the Prayers & Squares commandment against taking payment for a prayer quilt.

## Binky Patrol

http://www.binkypatrol.com

Begun in 1996 by a mother and daughter team who began stitching blankets and quilts for a local women's shelter, this nonprofit now has chapters nationwide. They distribute blankets, including quilts, to children ages 0 through 18 who are born with HIV/AIDS, drug or alcohol addictions, or are suffering with other chronic and terminal illnesses. They also give blankets to children who are abused, abandoned, are in foster care, or are experiencing trauma. They are based in Laguna Beach, California, and can be reached at 949-916-5926 or binky@binkypatrol.org.

## Lutheran World Relief

http://www.womenoftheelca.org/getinvolved/lwrquilts.html

This branch of the Evangelical Lutheran Church in America sends quilts, both quilted and tied, to needy people around the world. They request that quilts sent to them contain no religious iconography because they are sent to people of all faiths. Contact them in St. Paul, Minnesota, at 651-457-9009, or in New Windsor, Maryland, at 410-635-8798.

## My Brother's Keeper—Ugly Quilts

Started in 1985 on its founder's kitchen table, this charitable organization sews and distributes sleeping bags for the homeless made from discarded clothes and other fabrics. "Ugly" is a tongue-in-cheek reference to the results, which are often a patchwork of denim, flannel, fleece, and any other fabric as long as it is warm and soft. It is suggested that when the sleeping bags are rolled up, a "rolling prayer" is said: "Lord, take the work of our hands and bless it; and in Thy name let the person that receives this gift know that he is loved. Amen." It is based on a farm in Hop Bottom, Pennsylvania. Contact them at 570-289-4335.

## Newborns in Need

http://www.newbornsinneed.com

This Christian-based nonprofit provides clothing and other necessities, including quilts, to needy preemies and newborns and their families. Founded in 1992, it is based in Houston, Missouri, and has chapters across the country and in Puerto Rico. Contact them at 417-967-9441 or office@newsbornsinneed.org.

*Although the world is very full of suffering, it is also full of the overcoming of it.*

HELEN KELLER

*Most blest believer he!*

*Who in that land of
darkness and blind eyes*

*Thy long-expected
healing wings
could see,*

HENRY VAUGHAN*

## Project Linus

http://www.projectlinus.org

Located in Bloomington, Illinois, this nonprofit group provides blankets, including quilts, to pediatric cancer patients and children in trauma. Since their founding in 1995, they have given away over 1.2 million blankets from chapters all over the United States. Contact Project Linus at 309-664-7814 or information@projectlinus.org.

## QOV Foundation (Quilt of Valor)

http://www.qovf.org/index.html

Formerly "Quilts for Soldiers," this is a vast network of volunteers that aims to provide handmade quilts to every soldier wounded in the "war on terror," especially in Iraq and Afghanistan. They describe these quilts as their version of a Purple Heart medal. The quilts must measure at least 50 by 60 inches and should be quilted, not tied, and made of 100 percent cotton fabric. They also recommend quilters keep a written diary and take photos as they make a Quilt of Valor to share with the recipient. Contact persons and numbers are organized by geographic region and can be found on the group's website.

## Warming Families

http://www.warmingfamilies.org

This is a project of Strengthening Families, Alan and Suzanne Osmond's nonprofit organization that works to promote family life. They distribute blankets and other warm items to the homeless and displaced in the United States and Canada. Strengthening Families is based in Orem, Utah.

## Wrap Them In Love

http://wraptheminlove.org/

Based in Arlington, Washington, this nonprofit was founded in 1999 by a fabric store owner and quilter who adopted two children from a Korean orphanage. The group now collects quilts and distributes them to children in orphanages around the world. They welcome tied quilts. Contact them at admin@wraptheminlove.org.

There are other worthy charitable quilt and blanket organizations that could not be listed here. Some are national, and some operate on the local level. To find other organizations not listed here, visit About.com's page on charity and goodworks quilting, http://quilting.about.com/od/charityquilting/.

*The gloom of the world is but a shadow. Behind it, yet within reach, is joy. There is radiance and glory in the darkness, could we but see, and to see, we have only to look. I beseech you to look.*

Fra Giovanni

# AFTERWORD

At the beginning of this book, I said I had never needed a prayer quilt, thank goodness. As I put the finishing touches to the manuscript, that is no longer true.

Just as I was wrapping up this project, I went in for some minor surgery to repair a sinus cavity. I woke up in the day surgery center to see three or four nurses and doctors rushing about my bed, speaking very urgently, it seemed to me. I opened my mouth to speak and found that I could not take a breath. The next thing I knew, I was coughing up what seemed to me a lot of blood. I ended up spending the night in the hospital, taken there in a bumpy ambulance in the dark.

I was never in any real danger, but the whole experience scared me and my husband pretty badly. The complications and the night in the hospital started my recovery off very badly and I didn't bounce back as quickly as I would have hoped. I spent more than a week in bed.

Just as I was beginning to feel decent again, a package came in the mail. It was from someone in the San Diego area. I opened it up and out fell a gorgeous riot of color—a patch of blue and pink, two of my favorite colors. It was a prayer square that had been made for me by the prayer quilters at Foothills United Methodist Church.

That square of fabric touched me to my core. A writer's life is a lonely life. I spend most of my days alone in my office, connected to the world by technology—telephone, computer, and fax. This bit of cotton and thread leapt the distance between me and my friends in San Diego and made me feel loved, cherished, held dear—just as the yellow baby quilt of my childhood had.

I have since recovered fully from my surgery— and the flu and sinus infection that followed close on its heels. But I have not put aside the prayer square with the ibuprofen and the thermometer. It is here now, as I write. I keep it under my computer, confident that its prayers and good intentions will continue to embrace me in all that I do.

Kimberly Winston
Pinole, California
March 2006

*We must not, in trying to think about how we can make a big difference, ignore the small daily differences we can make which, over time, add up to big differences that we often cannot foresee.*

Marian Wright
Edelman

# NOTES

1. Sue Bender, *Everyday Sacred: A Woman's Journey Home* (San Francisco: HarperSanFrancisco, 1996).

2. George Atkin, "Holy Manna," in Benjamin Franklin White, *The Sacred Harp* (Reprint Services Corp., 1860).

3. Ole Hallesby, *Prayer* (Minneapolis: Augsburg Fortress, 1994; orig. pub. 1931).

4. Thomas Keating, *Open Mind, Open Heart* (New York: Continuum Publishing, 1994; orig. pub. 1986).

5. Tara Jon Manning, *Mindful Knitting: Inviting Contemplative Practice into the Craft* (Boston: Tuttle, 2004).

6. E. M. Bounds, *Purpose in Prayer* (New Kensington, Pa.: Whitaker House, 1997).

Unless otherwise noted, margin quotations have been excerpted from one of three sources:

* Robert Andrews, Mary Biggs, Michael Seidel, eds., *The Columbia World of Quotations* (New York: Columbia University Press, CD Rom edition, 1996).

** James B. Simpson, comp., *Simpson's Contemporary Quotations* (New York: Houghton Mifflin, 1988).

† John Bartlett, *Bartlett's Familiar Quotations: A Collection of Passages, Phrases and Proverbs Traced to Their Sources in Ancient and Modern Literature, 17th Edition* (New York: Little, Brown, 2002).

# BIBLIOGRAPHY

Atkins, Jacqueline Marx. *Shared Threads: Quilting Together Past and Present.* New York: Viking Studio Books, 1994.

Barbour, Russell, and Ruth Barbour. *Religious Ideas for Arts and Crafts.* Philadelphia: Christian Education Press, 1959.

Bender, Sue. *Everyday Sacred: A Woman's Journey Home.* San Francisco: Harper SanFrancisco, 1996.

———. *Plain and Simple: A Woman's Journey to the Amish.* San Francisco: HarperSanFrancisco, 1991.

Freedman, David Noel, ed. *Eerdmans Dictionary of the Bible.* Grand Rapids: William B. Eerdmans Publishing Company, 2000.

Goodwin, Debbie Salter. *Quilted with Love: Discovering the Patterns of Life's Grace and Beauty.* Colorado Springs: Honor Books, 2001.

Heim, Judy, and Gloria Hansen. *Free Stuff for Quilters on the Internet.* 3rd ed. Lafayette, Calif.: C&T Publishing, 2001.

Jorgensen, Susan S., and Susan S. Izard. *Knitting into the Mystery: A Guide to the Shawl Knitting Ministry.* Harrisburg, Pa.: Morehouse Publishing, 2003.

Koenig, Harold G. *The Healing Power of Faith: Science Explores Medicine's Last Great Frontier.* New York: Simon and Schuster, 1999.

Koenig, Harold G., Michael E. McCullough, and David B. Larson. *Handbook of Religion and Health.* New York: Oxford University Press, 2000.

Manning, Tara Jon. *Mindful Knitting: Inviting Contemplative Practice into the Craft.* Boston: Tuttle Publishing, 2004.

Mazloomi, Carolyn. *Spirits of the Cloth: Contemporary African American Quilts.* New York: Clarkson Potter, 1998.

———. *Threads of Faith: Recent Work from the Women of Color Quilters Network.* New York: American Bible Society, 2004.

Smith, Houston. *The World's Religions.* San Francisco: HarperSanFrancisco, 1991.

Towner-Larsen, Susan, and Barbara Brewer Davis. *With Sacred Threads: Quilting and the Spiritual Life.* Cleveland, Ohio: Pilgrim Press, 2000.